Discovering
Amphibians

Other books by John Himmelman

Discovering Moths: Nighttime Jewels in Your Own Backyard

Mouse in a Meadow

Frog in a Bog

Pipaluk and the Whales

The Animal Rescue Club

From the "Nature Up Close" series

A Wood Frog's Life
A Salamander's Life
A Mouse's Life
A Hummingbird's Life
A Monarch Butterfly's Life
A Ladybug's Life
A Luna Moth's Life
A Slug's Life

Discovering
Amphibians

Frogs and Salamanders
of the Northeast

John Himmelman

Photographs and Drawings
by the Author

Down East Books / Camden, Maine

For Betsy, who finds things . . .

Copyright © 2006 by John Himmelman. All rights reserved.
ISBN: 0-89272-703-9 13-digit 978-089272-703-2

Library of Congress Cataloging-in Publication:
Himmelman, John.
Discovering amphibians : frogs and salamanders of the Northeast /
JohnHimmelman ; photographs and drawings by the author.
p.   cm.
Includes bibliographical references and index.
ISBN 0-89272-703-9 (trade pbk. : alk. paper)
1. Frogs—Northeastern States. 2. Salamanders—Northeastern States.
I. Title.

QL668.E2H56 2006
597.80974—dc22
2005032712

Design by Faith Hague
Printed at Versa Press, E. Peoria, Ill.

2   4   5   3   1

Down East Books
A division of Down East Enterprise, Inc.
Publisher of *Down East*, the Magazine of Maine
Book orders: 1-800-685-7962
www.downeastbooks.com

Contents

Foreword

WHEN I WAS about seven years old, I found a pool of tadpoles in the sand at Jones Beach in Long Island, New York. I put them in my beach bucket and brought them home to a larger jar to see what they would turn into. I can still recall what they looked like—jet-black, almost all head, with skinny, pointy tails. Because I knew absolutely nothing about tadpoles, they starved to death in just a couple of days. Who would have thought they would actually need to eat?

This was my introduction to the world of amphibians. I'm afraid I didn't make a very good first impression. In the years that followed, I came across the occasional toad in the lawn or frog in the pond, but I really didn't think all that much about them.

In the mid-eighties, something happened that would set me on a course that continues to this day. My wife, Betsy, began painting watercolors of frogs. A high school art teacher, she is the most prolific artist I know, and I have come across quite a few. She will latch on to a new art form, master it, and create until her work spills out into every room in the house. Then she moves on to the next medium. Betsy always liked frogs, and when she began painting with watercolors, she chose them as her main focus. She would come home with stacks of books on the subject to use as

Betsy's painting of a wood frog

reference. She'd go out in the yard and photograph what she could find, and then paint from the photos. Our children were often called into service to pose for her, frog in hand. In short time, her paintings of these amphibians, both local and exotic, amassed in ever-growing stacks in the family room. Some she sold at local art shows while many were given away as gifts for special occasions. They adorned the walls of our home and the homes of friends and family. She didn't really care where they ended up; she just loved painting them, and I loved looking at them. Of all her incarnations as an artist, this was my personal favorite. Looking at her paintings, I grew to admire their subjects as art forms. Up until then, I had never thought of frogs that way.

Then, one afternoon, a wood frog appeared on our back deck. Betsy had recently completed a painting of one of these, and I looked at it as something I was already familiar with. But, instead of seeing it as represented in delicate washes of watercolor, I saw the frog itself. It sat on the deck plank like a squatting bulldog. The dark mask gave it the appearance that it was up to something, yet the pupils within those round eyes squinted in apparent aloofness. Its only movement was the steady pulsing of its throat. It truly was a work of art in and of itself. This time, *I* took some photos to try and capture what I was seeing. The photos weren't that great, so the next time I found a wood frog, I took some more. Though these photos were better, they still weren't as good as they could be. I soon found myself out looking for wood frogs. In doing so, I came across other frogs. They were interesting to look at, too, so I took more photos, telling myself that my wife could always use them. In reality, though, I was enjoying the hunt. The more frogs I found, the more I wanted to find, and I began to wonder just how many I *could* find in my area.

That hunt continues to this day, as does my quest to learn more about them. It was not a huge leap to acquire an appreciation for their cousins, the salamanders, as well. Salamanders have their own mystique and, to me, have always exuded a sense of being anchored in our primordial past. There is a simplicity in their form that I have since learned is anything but simple.

I have a driving urge to learn more about anything that interests me. While I make my living as an author and artist, I am also an interpretive naturalist. To put it simply, this is a person who finds some denizen of the natural world, researches and digests the scientific information about it, and then shares the more intriguing aspects with the general public. We naturalists all do this for the same reason: The lives and struggles taking place in our own backyards every minute of every day and night are as entertaining as the best movies out there. And for the same reason that people tend to like company when they go to the movies, we invite others to share in the appreciation of our outdoor discoveries. The enjoyment of a story, a song, a good meal, or an exciting find is enhanced when it can be shared. Betsy has long since moved on from painting frogs, but I continue to head out three seasons a year to find them. It is most fun when I am with friends who know how lucky we are to appreciate the free show running day and night in our ponds, forests, and fields.

This book is my way of inviting you to join us.

Now, let's roll some logs. . .

John Himmelman

Acknowledgments

I OWE THANKS to many people who have joined me in the field, shared some of their favorite amphibian spots, and provided me with photos to fill in some of the blanks in this book.

Among them are: Karro Frost (Mudpuppies! Finally!! Yeeha!!!); Hank Gruner for sending me to a great Jefferson salamander site; Noble Proctor (thanks for the springs and blue spots); and Bill Yule for sharing a great two-line and dusky salamander stream.

As my deadline loomed, I pestered these people to get some of the photos I needed: John Acorn (erythristic redback salamander); Billiam Kobak (his wife, Cindi, and their terrarium); Cindi Kobak (photo of their pond and of Frank Gallo); Frank Gallo (one of the Jefferson salamander shots); and Tom Tyning (Amherst tunnel, mink frog, and spadefoot toads).

Thank you also to John Ogren and Old Saybrook Troop 51 for letting me tag along on their salamander rescue event.

What Makes an Amphibian an Amphibian?

am- phib- i- an [amphibi-+*bios* life] *n* **1** animal or plant living
both on land and in water; **2** airplane designed to take off from
or land on water or land

THAT'S THE DEFINITION you get in the *Scribner-Bantam English Dictionary*. As you've most likely surmised, this book is not about airplanes.

Amphibians are divided into three major groups, or orders. Two of these, the Caudata (meaning "with tail"—salamanders) and the Anurans (meaning "without tail"—frogs), are represented in this book. The third, Caecilians (meaning "blind," referring to their small eyes), are limbless amphibians that live in tropical regions, so chances are you won't come across any in the wild here in the Northeast.

You may notice that the titles of many books about amphibians start with the words "Reptiles and." The names of these two classes—Reptilia and Amphibia—have been uttered in the same breath for close to a hundred years. In fact, prior to that, the Amphibia were lumped into the class of Reptilia, and many a layperson today still calls salamanders lizards and frogs reptiles. The reason these two groups are still studied together is mainly historical. Herpetologists still study both amphibians and reptiles, but many specialize in one or the other.

One way we avoid having to say "reptiles and amphibians," which is a mouthful, is to simply call them herps. People who study herps are herpetologists, and what they study is the herpetofauna. The practice of raising herpetofauna as pets is herpetoculture. The root of the word comes from the Greek word *herpes*, meaning "to creep." This form of locomotion was attributed to amphibians and reptiles, although certainly many do anything *but* creep. (Incidentally, the herpes virus is said to creep along neural pathways, hence the name. It has nothing to do with frogs and lizards.)

The traits amphibians and reptiles have in common, however, are not much different from what many other vertebrates share. In fact, reptiles share as many characteristics with birds as they do with amphibians. Oddly, a quick scan at the books in my library turned up no books titled *Reptiles and Birds*.

Amphibians and reptiles are both ectotherms, which means they lack the ability to hold their bodies at a constant temperature. This trait is commonly referred to as cold-blooded, but this is misleading. The only time an ectotherm's blood is cold is when the surrounding temperature is cold. The internal temperature of an ectotherm depends on an outside heat source. This explains why when you buy a lizard or frog at a pet store, at least here in the North, you usually have to buy a heat lamp, too.

The embryos of most species within the two classes also develop outside of the mother's body. In other words, they are egg layers, unlike the animals in the class Mammalia, which nourish their embryos within the mother's body and give birth to live young.

A case can be made for similarity in appearance between certain amphibians and reptiles. A quick glance at a lizard and a salamander shows them to share the same general shape: long bodies with legs coming out of the sides behind the neck and just before their tails. (Frog tails are reduced to internal rods called urostyles.) Their heads generally share the same proportion to those bodies, and species in both classes can bear a prominent set of eyes. An even stronger case can be made for similarities in appearance between tropical Caecilians and snakes, although, to my eye, the former more closely resemble large worms or millipedes than legless reptiles.

The two orders of Amphibia, Caudata and Anurans, to be explored in

The five-lined skink is the only lizard found in New England.

this book, share some common traits that are apparent to the casual observer. One trait is their smooth skin. Reptiles, which split off from the amphibians in the Carboniferous period, have skin covered in scales. This adaptation allowed them to expand their range to more arid habitats. The scales not only protect the skin, but also help prevent moisture loss. Since amphibians stay closer to water, their skin remains smooth. Amphibians still have to deal with the problem of dehydration, however, and have developed other strategies that allow for up to sixty-five percent water loss in the body, which we will examine further in the chapter "Frogsicles." Scales would also be an impediment to creatures that use their skin to absorb oxygen, as many amphibians do.

A look at the toes of an amphibian and a reptile will show another distinction between the two. Reptiles (snakes not withstanding) generally have claws. These are used for digging, climbing, and running. Amphibian toes are soft and blunt, with no claws or nails. While some, such as the spade-foot toad, do dig, they only excavate where the ground is soft or sandy. (I wonder if the lack of claws could also have something to do with their soft skin. Many amphibians get pretty physical when mating, and it's not hard to imagine injuries occurring if sharp objects were brought into the act.)

One major difference that sets amphibians apart from reptiles is how they bring their kind into the world. Reptiles lay eggs with hard shells. This is another adaptation that allows them to wander farther from water. The shells hold in moisture and nourishment, in the form of a yolk, long enough for the young reptile to develop within. When the reptile emerges, it resembles a miniature version of the adult.

Amphibians take a different route. Most lay their eggs in or near water. The eggs lack a hard protective shell, and the embryo emerges and develops in the surrounding water. This is the source of the name amphibian, which means "life on both sides." One side of that life is water; the other, once it has completed its larval stage, is land. The aquatic larval stage ranges from a couple of weeks to a couple of years. Young salamanders are called larvae. Young frogs are tadpoles or pollywogs. Tadpole basically means "toad head," which makes reference to its similarity in appearance to this part of the frog's anatomy. Pollywog means "wiggling head," again suggesting that it's basically a head with a tail. Some other names are polywig, porwiggle, and my favorite, porwiggy. Upon hatching, salamander larvae look similar to newly emerged tadpoles. Most, however, have a set of gills extending from the neck area.

Now that the obligatory differences between amphibians and reptiles have been pointed out, we can tuck this information away for a bit and concentrate on the differences and similarities between salamanders and frogs. It makes sense to begin with the Caudata, or salamanders, because they arrived here on earth before the frogs. About 536 species of sal-

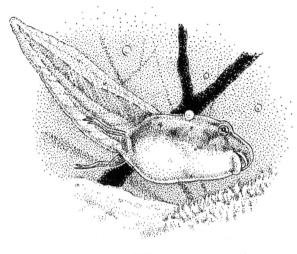

A wood frog tadpole

amanders exist worldwide (out of about 5,700 amphibians) with about 186 found from Canada to the southern North American border. In the Northeast , we have eighteen species. Each one is covered in more detail in the chapter titled "Species Accounts."

Salamanders are divided taxonomically into ten families based on their evolutionary relationships and anatomical features: Ambystomatidae (mole salamanders), Amphiumidae (amphiumas), Cryptobranchidae (giant salamanders and hellbenders), Dicamptodontidae (Pacific giant salamanders), Hynobiidae (Asian salamanders), Plethodontidae (lungless salamanders), Proteidae (mudpuppies and waterdogs), Rhyacotritonidae (torrent salamanders), Salamandridae (newts), and Sirenidae (sirens). Five of these families can be found in the Northeast: Ambystomatidae, Cryptobranchidne, Plethodontidae, Proteidae, and Salamandridae.

All of the salamanders within these four families, with the exception of the redback salamander, lay eggs in or near the water. The type of water body and/or surrounding habitat varies between the families and individual species. Prior to egg laying, some form of courtship usually happens between the males and females. This typically takes place in or near the breeding pool. Courtship rituals can include tail straddling, nudging, pushing, circling, chasing, tapping, stroking with teeth, scraping, and chin rubbing. A lot of this is brought on by, and initiates, a release of chemicals from glands in the cloaca, chin, cheeks, and other areas beneath the skin. These chemicals act as pheromones, creating a love potion to woo the opposite sex. Pheromones not only stimulate the drive to reproduce, they help animals determine that their suitors are within the same species. Mating with species other than their own is not only unproductive, it is also a waste of valuable breeding time.

After finding a taker, the male ejects a spermatophore through his cloaca. The cloaca, present in both males and females, technically means "sewer," or at least that's the Latin root of the word. In animals such as amphibians, birds, and fish, it is a posterior opening through which they evacuate wastes and deposit (males) or receive (females) reproductive material. It is also known as the vent. In salamanders, the reproductive material comes in a packet known as a spermatophore, which is a small gelatinous structure containing a packet of sperm at the top. The male plants his spermatophore, often several, on the strata in front of the female. The female straddles one of the packets and picks it up through her cloaca. Sometimes she takes just the sperm-filled packet at the top; sometimes she picks up the whole package. The sperm is then stored in her spermatheca, a chamber connected to the cloaca. When she is ready to deposit her eggs, they pass through that area and become fertilized.

Eggs are laid in a variety of ways: singly, in clusters, attached to vegetation, loose on the pond floor, under rocks and decaying logs, in moss, beneath leaves, and in underground cavities. Wherever they end up, they need to stay damp, as there is no shell to hold in moisture to stave off desiccation. Instead, a flexible vitelline membrane surrounds the eggs. This is often clear, and the developing embryo can be observed within. In a number of species, the mother will wrap her body around the eggs to keep them moist and protect them from predators. The male, however, typically bids the female a sweet *adieu* after courtship and takes no part in looking after his offspring.

Regardless of whether or not the eggs are attended to by the female, once the young hatch, they're on their own. If they hatch on land, as many of the Plethodons do, they have to make it to the water. If they hatch in the water, they are where they are going to be until they develop into the juvenile salamander. There are exceptions. Mudpuppies remain aquatic throughout their lives and some Plethodons have populations or individuals that are also neotonic, which means that they retain their larval characteristics into adulthood. Red-spotted newts develop in the water, move out to the land, and then return to the water to stay. Redback salamanders go through their larval stage within eggs laid in a rotting log.

Salamander larvae start out looking like tadpoles with gills (bear in mind that some tadpoles have gills, too). Those gills can look like a tangle of tendrils, or sea fans, and they radiate from the sides of the head. In species that inhabit moving streams, the gills tend to be shorter and less bushy, and those which breed in still water have longer, bushier gills. In the case of the former, because they live in water that offers more oxygen, they don't have to work as hard to absorb this gas. Therefore, the structures responsible for doing this need not be as prominent. (I also wonder if larger gills would make navigation more difficult in a current.) The species living in standing or turbid water don't have as much oxygen available to them. A mechanism that provides more surface area for oxygen absorption would be very helpful. Mudpuppies, who can live in extremely muddy water, have gills that make it look as if the sides of their head exploded. Their gills resemble big purple cheerleader pompoms.

Some salamander larvae have fleshy appendages, or balancers, emanating from the sides of the head. A newly hatched larva cannot swim very well, and these balancers, which are gone in a few days, keep it from spinning out of control.

Salamander larvae are predators within their world. Prior to the appearance of limbs, they feed on tiny crustaceans and other aquatic invertebrates. As they grow larger, and their limbs and digits develop, they become more adept at snagging larger prey. Some even become cannibalistic, especially in conditions where there is more competition for food. I have come across many a salamander larva, mostly in the Ambystomid family, with parts of its tail, or even legs, bitten off. But the larvae have more to fear than each other. They are mostly nocturnal, which reduces some predation, but giant water bugs, diving beetles, water scorpions, frogs, turtles, raccoons, birds, and fish are among the many creatures that devour them. If they survive these predators, the larvae transform into juveniles. At first, juveniles stick around their natal habitats. They generally keep out of sight and remain beneath the moist soil and leaves. As they adapt more fully to the terrestrial world, they disperse from the ponds, lakes, and streams. Some

A spotted salamander larva catching a copepod

return to live along the pond edge; some colonize new habitats. I have created a few new vernal pools. They have always been found and used for breeding by several species of salamanders within a year of their making. This is evidence that the juveniles' wanderlust pays off in expanding their territories and establishing new colonies.

Adult salamanders spend their lives under things—leaves, logs, and rocks, mostly. While they may not have the need to keep their bodies submerged, they still have to keep their skin moist. The damp medium facilitates oxygen absorption and waste gas expulsion through the skin. Some salamanders prefer a semiaquatic habit and live right along the edges of streams. Others, such as the Ambystomids, live in upland forest areas. Nearly all are nocturnal. This helps them remain hidden from predators, such as birds and snakes, and prevents the loss of moisture to the sun. Rainy nights bring them to the surface to hunt various invertebrates.

Salamanders do not have the capacity to elicit fear in a creature larger than they are. They have no claws to scratch with; they have no fangs to bite with; they can't throw rocks or kick sand in the face. What many of them do have is a really bad taste. In fact, a number of species are downright toxic. The toxicity is usually just in the skin, so birds and mammals often eat roadkills, which offer the innards without having to go through what contains them. The toxins are in mucus produced by granular glands just beneath the surface of the skin. This mucus serves to retain moisture, and because it is usually high in proteins, it can help supplement nourishment during periods of food shortage.

Some species offer their tail to the predator as a compromise. This defense mechanism is known as tail autotomy. Once the tail is fully detached, it keeps moving; this movement is key in holding the attention of the hunter. While the predator is fixated on the moving tail, the salamander tiptoes away. Eventually, the salamander will grow a new one.

Because salamanders cannot freeze (well, they can, but it kills them), they need to spend the winter somewhere relatively warm to escape the ice and snow. Typically, this is within a burrow beneath the leaf litter or in the damp mud along their aquatic, or semiaquatic, habitat. Having no claws, they have to find a burrow that is ready-made, although they do have a modicum of capacity for improving it. As soon as the danger of freezing has passed, they exit these burrows to either breed or pick up where they left off the previous fall.

The salamander life span varies with the species, and generally ranges between three and thirty years. This is quite a bit longer than the life span of frogs, which probably has about as much to do with the salamander's cryptic behavior as the physiological differences between the two.

●

And now, on to the frogs.

More than five thousand species of frogs exist in the world, with ninety-five species occurring north of the Mexican border. With the exception of Antarctica, they are found everywhere on the planet. If you were to check these species numbers in a field guide written twenty years ago, you would notice that they have nearly doubled. Of course those frogs were always there, but our ability to sort through them continues to improve, and we keep coming across previously undescribed species. Many of these new frogs are discovered in tropical areas.

The Northeast is home to fourteen species of frogs belonging to four of the thirty families found throughout the world. The Northeastern families are Pelobatidae (spadefoot toads), Ranidae (true frogs), Bufonidae (toads), and the Hylidae (treefrogs).

The metamorphosis process for frogs is similar to that of salamanders. They, too, go through the stages of egg, larva, juvenile, and adult. Aside from some of the morphological features, what truly set them apart from their salamander cousins are two things: They make noise and they hop. Both of these traits are what come to mind when we hear the word *frog*. Noise making, or, to be more accurate, calling, is something the frog does to define and defend territory, signal distress, thwart unwanted amorous advances, and court the opposite sex, which brings to mind an old ditty:

There was an old frog lived in a well
Ding! Dang! Dong! go the Wedding Bells
A pretty little mouse lived in a mill
Ding! Dang! Dong! go the Wedding Bells
Froggy went a courting and he did ride
Ding! Dang! Dong! go the Wedding Bells
He said "Missy Mouse you must decide"
Ding! Dang! Dong! go the Wedding Bells . . .

This song, "The Frog's Courtship" or "Froggy Went a-Courting," has been around in a variety of forms for roughly four hundred years. While frogs don't court mice (some are known to eat them), it is the courtship of the frog that draws our attention. Those of us who live where there are frogs can't *help* but notice it. In the Northeast, nights in our woods and meadows are virtually silent throughout the winter months. Aside from the owls and the occasional coyote, there's really nothing to hear but the neighbors' dogs barking. But come spring, that silence is broken by the calls of wood frogs and spring peepers. These are soon followed by the calls of the pickerel frogs, American toads, Fowler's toads, and so on. Because we won't be hearing any insects until the spring field crickets let loose in May, the frogs steal the show. No, they *are* the show.

While, to us, the peeps, quacks, groans, and trills add a welcome aural texture to the night's mosaic, for the frogs, it is serious business. Frogs call with the help of a patch, or two patches, of skin called vocal sacs. These fill with air and act as echo chambers as that air passes over the vocal cords. The males do most of the calling, and the louder the sound, the farther it will carry to lure in females. The serenading usually takes place in or near where the females' eggs will be laid. Some frogs, such as the Hylidae, call from trees and vegetation surrounding the water. Other frogs call while floating on the surface, partially submerged, or under the water. Pickerel frogs serenade underwater, and, amazingly, their groaning calls can still be heard from quite a distance from the ponds or lakes. Calling from underwater is probably the safest way to court the females, as frog calls also attract predators. In some areas, where frogs have taken up residence along noisy rivers, they forgo the vocalizations, which would only be drowned out. Instead, they wave their legs in the air as if they're hailing a taxi.

●

Animals designed to communicate aurally must be able to hear sound as well as produce it. The ears of frogs, known as the tympanum, are sometimes quite obvious to the observer. They are located behind the eyes and what we actually see are the tympanic membranes. The membrane is a thin, round layer of skin that vibrates in response to sound and sends the signals to the eardrum. In many species, the size of the tympanic membrane can be used to determine the sex of the frog. In males, they are somewhat larger than the diameter of the eye. In the females, they are about the same size or smaller. I came up with a mnemonic to help me remember which is which: MALE—Males Are Large-Eared. This works better for me than my first attempt: FEMALE—Females Embarrassingly Model A Lesser Ear, which is just plain ridiculous.

A look at the tympanic membrane of a male green frog

Many frogs practice what is known as chorusing. Again, the males do this, and it is, in effect, a synchronized advertisement call. (Incidentally, a group of frogs is called a chorus.) Calling together creates a huge beacon of sound, making it easier for the females to locate the males. Studies suggest that chorusing arises from male competition. In their attempt to outdo each other, they join in song. Once the females arrive to the chorusing site, they choose which male they will mate with, often by virtue of the quality of his song. Some insects—snowy tree crickets, for example—employ this same chorusing technique to draw in females.

Calling requires a huge amount of energy. Some frogs, known as satellite males, conserve their energy by not calling at all. Instead, the little sneaks position themselves near a caller to intercept a responsive female. This technique, however, does not prove to be as successful as does the actual calling.

The female usually selects the mate by signaling to that male that he's the lucky one. This is often accomplished with a touch or by assuming the position. The male climbs on to the female's back and grabs her just behind the front legs. (Some, such as the spadefoot toads, grab behind the hind legs.) Many frogs develop a tubercle, a hardened protruberance on the thumb, to aid in holding on to the female while mating. Sometimes several males will fight over a mate. The males give release calls, basically to tell the other males, "Get off me." In the heat of sexual frenzy, though, these calls can be ignored, and in some instances, when so many males pile onto a single female, she can drown.

As with salamanders, fertilization is external. The male adds his sperm as the eggs leave the female. Also similar to salamanders, the eggs can be laid singly, in clusters, loose in the water, or attached to vegetation. Toads lay their eggs in long chains. When the eggs hatch, tadpoles will either drop to the pond floor or linger on the egg mass. At this point, many tadpoles have external gills, similar to those in newly hatched salamanders. Within a few days, the gills become internal. New tadpoles are very weak swimmers, so they remain relatively still to avoid drawing attention from predators. Some will feed on algae that grew on the egg mass during incubation. A sucker-like mouth enables them to attach themselves to their food as they graze.

Tadpoles are food for so many creatures, it's amazing that any of them make it out of the water. They do, though, and that's because their large numbers offset their propensity to be eaten. In fact, their numbers are so large that if even half of the tadpoles survived to adulthood, we'd be tripping over frogs everywhere we went.

Frog tadpoles are mainly herbivores, feeding on algae and other aquatic plants. They also eat detritus and, on occasion, other tadpoles and the eggs of other frog species. Their rate of development varies with the habitats in which they are found. The amount of food they eat also affects how long they remain in the larval stage. The more they find, the faster they grow. After awhile, their legs develop from tiny leg buds found on the outside of the body. Typically, the back legs form first, then the front legs. As they grow, the tail is absorbed into the body, which helps provide additional nutrients during their transformation from herbivore to insectivore. Prior to leaving the water as a newly metamorphosed froglet, they stop eating.

In addition to changing from herbivore to insectivore and from a wriggler to a hopper, they also forgo the use of internal gills in exchange for the lungs of a terrestrial, or semiterrestrial, frog. Air is pumped into the lungs by the throat muscles in a mechanism known as buccal pumping. That's why a frog's throat is always pulsating. (In mammals, it is the ribs you notice expanding and contracting as breathing takes place. Frogs have ribs, but they are reduced and attached to the vertebrae. Salamanders lack ribs entirely.) Buccal pumping is not an efficient way to take in oxygen, so frogs supplement this by exchanging gases through the skin, which has a vast network of blood vessels for that purpose.

While salamanders sometimes retain their larval qualities, frogs always complete the full metamorphosis from tadpole to the typical adult frog form. The young froglets stay relatively close to home as they absorb the rest of their tail and develop their new insectivore skills. Once the tail is fully absorbed, they closely resemble the adults, although colors and patterns may be different to aid in camouflage.

I've always thought of this change from larva to adult, which takes between a few months and a few years, as an accelerated process of evolution. Hundreds of millions of years ago, the creatures of the sea made a similar change; they developed from water breathers to air breathers. However, that evolutionary step occurred over millions of years. This impression of evolution played at fast-forward is bolstered by the similarity in appearance of the new "metamorphs" to that of the earliest frogs.

Though tadpoles and salamander larvae share many characteristics, the adult forms are structurally quite different. One difference lies in the backbone. In frogs, the posterior three or four vertebrae are fused, forming a urostyle. This structure, along with the pelvis, provides strength and stiffness to the rear of the body, where the muscles used for jumping are attached to the skeleton. Imagine the world of pain you would be in if you had to bounce across the ground on your coccyx. Add to that an exponentially increased adeptness at jumping provided by a pair of elongated, well-muscled legs. What goes up must come down, and the added backbone strength and flexibility compensate for that.

Frogs jump to escape danger, to lunge at prey, and to get from one place to another. Those long hind legs also come in handy for swimming, and frogs often escape danger by jumping into the water. If you walk along a pond's edge and startle a frog, you'll hear a short alarm call and then a splash. Once in the water, they give a couple kicks with those powerful legs and are hiding in the muck of the pond's floor in no time. Because many live in open areas, I imagine that hopping is the fastest way to get from one end of the field to the other while drawing the least amount of attention. A steady crawling motion allows more time for a predator to locate you. When you jump and then stop, jump and then stop, there are longer moments when you are motionless and blending in with the background. This increases the chances for a predator to move on to something else that is still moving. Toads, on the other hand, do crawl, but they are poisonous so would fare better if discovered. That poison is produced by their parotoid glands and can be quite toxic.

Frogs tend to be nocturnal for the same reasons as salamanders: The sun can dry out skin that needs to remain moist, and fewer predators are about at night. Their patterns and coloration are designed to make frogs blend in with their habitat, so different habitats produce different-looking frogs. Frogs that spend time among leaves in the woodland or forest canopy are usually green, and frogs that live on the ground are the colors of that ground or the leaf litter—browns, black, and ochre. Some species show a range of colors and patterns among individuals, which can make it difficult for a predator to learn to recognize what it's supposed to be looking for. An exception can be found in the poisonous species. They want every predator to know they are inedible, and they advertise this with an array of bright contrasting colors.

You will not find frogs or salamanders roaming too close to salt water. As with slugs, salt desiccates their bodies. To aid in their nonending quest to remain moist, the Anurans produce liquid through granular glands beneath the skin, which is where the toxins are located in most species. All frogs produce toxins from these glands, as do all salamanders. However, in most species the toxin is so weak that it is no deterrent to predatory birds, fish, and mammals (including humans). The main purpose of the glands is to keep the skin moist. The toxins, in their varying strengths, came as an offshoot of the chemicals used to remain hydrated and provide backup proteins during periods of low food supply.

A frog makes its living hunting worms, insects, slugs, spiders, minnows, sowbugs—pretty much anything that will fit into its wide mouth. After locating a potential meal, the frog lunges at it and flips out its long, sticky tongue. Once in the mouth, the prey goes straight down to the stomach—whole. While frogs do have teeth, they are too tiny to deal with chewing. Plus, they're located only on the roof of the mouth, making grinding the food impossible. If you watch a frog swallow, you will notice that its eyes sink down into its head during that process. Muscles attached to the backs of the eyes actually push the food down the throat.

A frog's vision is sharp, and the location of its eyes on the sides of the head gives it great depth perception. Frogs see well, but what causes them to lunge has more to do with the movement of its prey than what that prey looks like. I discovered this while fishing for green frogs and bullfrogs at the edge of a pond. If you take a long piece of grass with a prominent seed head and dangle it in front of a frog, it will lunge at the grass and take it in its mouth. You can actually lift the frog off the ground while it is still holding onto the grass. You would think a creature that lives among the grasses and sedges at the edge of a pond could distinguish between a piece of grass and a caterpillar, especially in light of those large, all-seeing eyes, but apparently the movement of the grass overrides all other visual input and triggers the "looks good to eat, so I'm gonna" response. This should not be big news to cat owners. Cats, too, have great vision, but they can be stimulated to attack just about anything based on how it moves.

(Incidentally, I really don't pick on frogs in this manner often, because I feel guilty afterward. If someone did that to me with a rubber pizza, I'd be pretty ticked off.)

When frogs are thirsty, they, like any animal, need to find water, but when it comes to liquid replenishment, they act more like plants. Frogs and salamanders don't drink. Instead, they find a pool of water, sit in it, and absorb the liquid through the skin of their belly and legs. In fact, both can even extract water from damp sand, mud, and dew-covered rocks.

As the weather grows colder, Northeastern Anurans begin to grow large and sluggish as fat gets stored in a special gland in the abdomen. This will be their food supply throughout the winter. To preserve energy, biological functions slow down, including digestion. A chilled frog cannot eat.

Frogs select a place, known as a hibernaculum, in which to spend the winter. Most of them have to, to avoid freezing. For some species, the hibernaculum is a shelter within the muck at the bottom of a lake or pond. Others, such as the wood frog, spring peeper, and gray treefrog, can freeze solid, so their choice of shelter need not be more than a pile of leaves, a shallow burrow, or a crevice beneath a rotten log. All frogs, whether they can survive freezing or not, produce a good amount of antifreeze to protect their cells and organs from the onslaught of ice crystals. This cryoprotectant is most often in the form of glucose and, sometimes, alcohol.

Frogs remain inactive throughout winter and begin to stir when the temperature consistently reaches the high thirties to low forties Fahrenheit. Rain, length of day, and barometric pressure also play a role in awakening them from their slumber. Those frogs which overwinter farther from the surface wake later; it takes them a bit longer to get the message that spring is on its way.

Frogs generally don't live more than three to five years. So many things out there like to eat them that it is likely very few die of old age.

$\backsim$ 2 $\backsim$

From Amphibians to Us

THE NEXT TIME you have the opportunity, pick up a salamander and have a good look at one of its hands. It looks familiar. Aside from having one less finger, it looks much like what encloses your subject—jointed fingers radiating from a fleshy palm. We have something in common with the amphibians: hands—grasping hands, propelling hands, pushing hands, stabilizing hands. Your hand and the hand you are looking at are legacies from a shared ancestor—an amphibian.

As you know, we didn't always look the way we do. We share the same humble beginnings with every terrestrial vertebrate on this planet. In fact, our origins are shared by every living thing existing above and below the surface of the planet. However, a special tip of the hat goes to the pioneering amphibians that were the first vertebrates to leave the water. We are what they have become.

The earth is about 4.55 billion years old and for the first billion years it sat lifeless. Those who ascribe to the Gaia Hypothesis, that the earth itself is a living creature, may wonder if our orb looks back on those quiet days with fondness. In reality, those times were anything but peaceful. The roiling, unstable, meteor-bombarded state our planet was in prevented any form of life. While this provided building blocks for the chemicals that would eventually combine to create life, things had to settle a bit first.

Our most distant ancestors first appeared during the Proterozoic eon, about 2.5 billion years ago. How long it took for that first instance of life to appear is unknown. Some paleontologists say it took more than a billion years for the chemicals in the ocean to combine to form what we consider a living organism. Others say that in a young, unstable earth, a billion years is too long of a time period. Things would be going along nicely for, say, two or three hundred million years only to be wiped out by yet another giant meteor. They believe that life would have happened in a relatively short amount of time, perhaps less than 20 million years, and that it had to be the result of a chance event—or a series of them.

However long it took, it is generally believed that various chemicals got together to form our great-to-the-umpteenth-power grandparents—single-celled blue-green algae. If you think that we have a great effect on our planet's environment today, it is nothing when compared with that of our microscopic forebears. These algae spread throughout the oceans and developed a way to capture energy from our sun. One of the by-products of this metabolism was, and is, free oxygen. There had to be a lot of algae out there to create oxygen in such a substantial amount, though they did have millions of years to accomplish this. Maybe the next time you are scraping that green stuff off the side of your aquarium, you will appreciate the contribution algae have made to life on earth. Not only are algae the oldest form of life in the solar system, they are also responsible for all the forms that followed. Before algae, our atmosphere was a mix of unbreathable gases—hydrogen, carbon monoxide, methane, ammonia, and so on. This was in no small part a result of all the planet's volcanic activity. The addition of oxygen allowed for a quantum leap in the evolution of life.

Now that life had a foot in earth's door, it did what life is renowned for doing—it multiplied, mutated, and branched. The Phanerozoic era, 540 to one million years ago, saw an explosion of more complex creatures. Within that era was the Cambrian period, which occurred between 540 and 510 million years ago. Life was evolving into all kinds of forms, from jellyfishlike trilobozoans to the fierce, two-foot long, razor-toothed shrimp called Anomalocaris.

This is also the time period that gave us the *Pikaia*, a two-inch worm believed to be a precursor to all vertebrates. We are moving up in the world; we have gone from algae to worm. What makes this creature so special is that it is the first to show the characteristics of the group known as the chordates. We

Pikaia, *the first known precursor to the vertebrates*

are chordates. Among the features that make a chordate are: a spinal cord that generally gets larger toward the head, with the larger end containing sensory organs; a blood system that travels through a tubular network; kidneys; a pharynx; and a particular type of musculature. While there are not enough well-preserved fossils to truly get to know this creature, there are enough to determine that it had some of these traits, and to date, that it is the first known creature to exhibit them.

The chordates branched into three different groups. One group became sea squirts, marine creatures that start out as tadpolelike larvae and then become sedentary, almost plantlike, adults. Another group includes the Branchiostoma, eel-like animals that burrow in the mud in shallow water and feed by way of short tentacles surrounding the mouth. Vertebrates are the third subphylum, and it is this group that eventually grew jaws and then teeth. This is an important step from our perspective, as it allowed for a greater selection of food, and in many cases, better defense. It also increased vertebrates' success as predators.

What they needed now was a better way to propel themselves through the water, and a way to keep from sinking now that they had grown these big, heavy heads. The development of a different set of appendages solved this problem and eventually brought them out of the water. Fins became important adaptations for creatures with dense muscles and heavy bones. They not only aided in propulsion and steering, but kept vertebrates from sinking to the bottom. These fins, particularly the fleshy or lobe-finned variety, were the precursor to what I am using to type these words, and you are using to flip the pages in this book.

Where does that lead us now? From algae to worm to fish? It would appear so, naturally with many interesting steps in between. However, the development of a particular type of fin was needed to pull us out of the water. The sarcopterygians, which appeared on the scene about 400 million years ago in the Early Devonian period, had such appendages. These fins were fleshy, muscular, and were reinforced with bone. Looking at their structure, it is not a far leap to see a resemblance to the structure of our own hands and feet. The location of these fins, fore and aft, also helps one visualize where limbs would develop on their terrestrial descendants, and on those which have returned to the sea, such as whales and dolphins.

Two of these lobe-finned fish have survived millions of years virtually unchanged—the coelacanth and the lungfish. I'm sure you've heard of the coelacanth, which was thought to have become extinct 65 million years ago but was rediscovered by a trawler off the coast of South Africa in 1938. It's a big fish, measuring about six feet long. Its fins contain bones that are similar to those of another fish, the *Eusthenopteron*, which has been credited as the closest precursor to the first terrestrial vertebrates. (More on that one shortly.) While the coelacanth does not use its fins for walking, its appearance 400 million years ago shows that evolution was starting to *think* about making that leap. The coelacanth's fins can be viewed as preadaptations to leaving the water.

Lungfish are still found in South America, Australia, and Africa. Their lungs evolved from what was originally a buoyancy organ called a swim bladder. The swim bladder has been absorbing oxygen for these fish since the Devonian period. This adaptation allows them to breathe in their muddy burrows when their pools are dry.

Lungfish are believed by some to be the closest living relatives of the amphibians that eventually left the water, and they share some important characteristics with them. They have the ability to breathe through lungs and have a similar arrangement of limbs. A recent study suggests that we possess a physical throwback to these ancient creatures—the hiccup. According to an Australian team of scientists led by Christian Straus, of Pitie-Salpetriere Hospital in Paris, the circuitry of the hiccup is something we have retained from the first air-sucking creatures. The hiccup served as a building block for more complex motor patterns that allow us to keep food out of the windpipe and enable nursing infants to breathe while feeding. Mothers and pregnant women can attest to the fact that babies hiccup even before their lungs are fully developed. Could what takes place during gestation be a dramatically accelerated echo of the evolutionary process? If so, does the prenatal hiccup represent the kick-start of the breathing mechanism, which occurred along the evolutionary line?

In their journal *BioEssays* the Paris researchers wrote, "Hiccups may be the price to pay to keep this useful pattern generator." Something we can all confirm is how hard it is to stop the hiccups once they begin. For us, it is an annoying occurrence, but for a fish just starting out with a new set of supplementary lungs, this reflex could have played a large role in making the transition. Lungfish were required to force the air into their lungs while simultaneously utilizing their gills. A hiccup causes an abrupt constriction of the diaphragm, forcing the hiccupper to take in a gulp of air; at the same time, it closes the glottis, the space between the vocal folds. This occurs in a repetitive pattern that is not as comfortable and consistent as our normal breathing pattern. In fact, these hiccups behave in an almost desperate manner. In a way, it is extreme breathing.

Some paleontologists point to yet another fish, this one fully extinct, which may hold the distinction of being the true ascendant of amphibians. It is called *Eusthenopteron*. Detailed study of the fossils show what could be a humerus attached to a shoulder, and two forearm bones, the ulna and radius. Within the rear fins was a femur attached to a pelvis, and on the end of the femur were the tibia and fibula. The rear fins could be used for both swimming and walking. They contained the components to build hands and feet and the supporting arms and legs as well. Eusthenopteron also had lungs, which is crucial if you are going be spending any time with your head above water. And this fish may very well have suffered and/or benefited from the hiccups. Not only did the *Eusthenopteron* have air-breathing pouches like the lungfish and the fleshy-fin structure of both the lungfish and coelacanth, it also had an additional adaptation missing in both of its contemporaries: a passage that links the nostrils with the roof of the mouth. This arrangement is present in all land-dwelling vertebrates.

Whichever one of these three lobe-finned fish took the next step up for the vertebrates—or even if it was another yet to be discovered species, or several—it would appear that, structurally, we were ready to go.

•

While all these changes were taking place, other momentous events were occurring in our growing world. For one, plants were appearing on land— simple algae at first, but by about 440 million years ago, more complex plants had arrived. Ferns, club mosses, lichens, and fungi dominated. During that time, in the Early Silurian period, invertebrate creatures— mollusks, crustaceans, worms, centipedes, millipedes, spiders, scorpions, and early forms of insects—left the lakes and seas. These early animal colonizers had to be in place before the arrival of the vertebrates; after all, they were to be their food.

All of this brings us finally to our first terrestrial ancestor—the amphibian. These ancient amphibians are known more accurately as tetrapods, which means "four-footed" animals. The earliest fossils showing legs suitable for life on land were found in Greenland. Three species are in evidence, ranging in size between two and four feet long, and they lived during the Upper Devonian period, about 350 million years ago.

Little is known about one of them, *Ichthyostegopsis*, of which only a skull fossil has been found, but the other two have been well studied. *Ichthyostega*

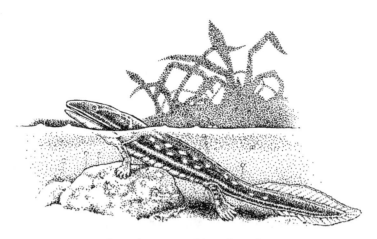

Acanthostega *taking a breather*

was a three-and-a-half-foot-long creature with a large head, four limbs, and a fishlike tail. Its forelegs were robust, and it is believed that they were able to support the weight of the front of its body. On land, however, it most likely dragged itself along; the back legs do not appear to have had the strength to lift the middle and rear sections of the body.

Acanthostega, about half the length of *Ichthyostega* and of a slenderer build, had weak limbs that could support very little of its body weight. Still, they would have been superior to fins for moving about in shallow water. On its undersides Acanthostega also had a protective layer of scutes, which were not present anywhere else on the body. This would suggest an adaptation to prevent abrasion when it slid about. *Acanthostega*, in addition to using lungs, still retained its internal gills. It could breathe above and below the water's surface, which made it a true transitional form.

Tetrapods were more fish than amphibian and more at home in water than on land. It is likely that they spent most of their time in shallow water, where they were active hunters. Their lives can be compared with today's mudskippers. (While they are in a different group than the early tetrapods, mudskippers have the ability to gain land for short amounts of time even though they are primarily aquatic creatures.)

The amphibians that followed were generally large, between one and fifteen feet long. They had heavy skeletons and strong arms and legs. What they shared with our modern amphibians was limited, though. The ancient tetrapods relied on water as the medium in which to lay their eggs. So, too, do our modern frogs and salamanders. Of course there are exceptions with some of today's species, but the generalization holds true. The tetrapods lived in and out of the water, as do the amphibians of today. Remember, the word amphibian means "life on both sides," and most of the ancient variety lived such a life. They were and are both active predators as well; they never evolved the teeth, jaw, and digestive system needed to process plants as food.

Unlike the skin of modern amphibians, tetrapod skin was tough. Many tetrapods retained their fishy scales to protect their bodies in the harsh new world. This means that they must have had lungs, because a tough body covering would not facilitate skin breathing. The skin of modern amphibians is smooth and used to supplement the lungs (in the amphibians that have them) in oxygen absorption. Without rib cages, lung breathing is less efficient, and our frogs and salamanders either lack this structure or possess it in reduced form. Compared with their tetrapod ancestors, they also have relatively feeble bones.

Unlike many of the early tetrapods, most of our amphibians are small. This is the result of having evolved to be dependent on skin breathing. The larger the creature, the greater the body volume requiring oxygen. Yes, the skin covering would be larger, too, but not in a proportion that would allow that process to work efficiently. Maximum skin area and minimum body size formed the most successful formula.

But why would these early amphibians leave the water? There is a reason for every action and adaptation made throughout the course of evolution, and generally, each reason points to an advantage gained by each change. Living in the water offered tremendous benefits. A major plus had to do with the reduction of gravity's effect on a body. Fish could grow very large in the seas and lakes. On land, such great sizes would mean an increase in body weight, and without proper skeletal support, the organs would be crushed under the weight of the body.

In the water, temperatures remain relatively stable compared with the surface. Changes that do occur take place more slowly and less dramatically. This reduces the need for a water dweller to regulate its own body temperature, which is another plus. The water also envelops its creatures with the essential gases and nutrients needed for respiration and growth. In addition, water provides a medium in which to reproduce, allowing for the transfer of sexual elements. Why would any creature want to leave all this behind?

Three theories have been proposed to explain how, and why, fish grew legs. One of the earliest theories suggests that it was a result of the periodic drying of lakes and ponds; a fish that could breathe air and hunt for food in new habitats would have an edge on the ones that . . . well, died.

Another theory suggests that the biggest obstacle for fish survival in those times was not the drying of the lakes, but stagnation. This is a condition that still occurs all over the world, most frequently in tropical areas. A stagnant lake is very low in oxygen. A fish that could move to a more suitable habitat would have a definite advantage in bringing more of its kind into the world. Consequently, certain fish developed legs to take them to new habitats and lungs to allow them to spend more time on land as they traveled.

The last theory suggests that the early amphibian adaptations were meant to aid the creatures in the water, not on land. An animal living in the shallows could use those legs to push its head above the surface to supplement its oxygen intake. Feet would allow it to grab onto the bottom to hold itself in place and would also help to propel it as it hunted for food. As someone who has done a bit of snorkeling, I can picture this scenario. A snorkeler looking for fish and coral in shallow water will move along the bottom by pulling his or her body along with the hands. The feet are used as fins to gain an extra burst of speed or power when needed. *Ichthyostega* and *Acanthostega* probably moved about in this way. This last theory allows the tetrapods to evolve where they are. It is supported by the earliest fossil records, which show tetrapods to be more fish than amphibian.

David Norman discusses this theory in his book *Prehistoric Life, the Rise and Fall of Vertebrates*. He disagrees with scientists who view the changes in tetrapod physiology as adaptations to deal with life on land, asserting instead that those changes emerged as a way to cope with the swampy conditions of the Devonian period. He speculates that tetrapods only reluctantly made the move from water to land.

I like his choice of that word *reluctantly*. This would dispel any notion that these creatures had a desire to leave the comforts of home. There was no amphibian Manifest Destiny or land rush. When things got bad for them, they did what they had to do, even if that meant pushing themselves into the harsh terrestrial environment. And they did so while still keeping one foot in the water for as long as they possibly could.

Over time, the early amphibians' foothold on dry land grew stronger. That land was forming into the supercontinent known as Pangaea, and it offered opportunities and safety not found in the sea. During the Carboniferous period, which occurred between 360 and 286 million years ago, plant life exploded, creating forests and swamps. Trees and insects dominated the air, but amphibians ruled the earth. These were not the plucky little spring peepers you and I are familiar with. These were powerful animals with strong limbs and sharp teeth. They could grow to more than fifteen feet long and, as with their early predecessors, their skin was tough, and some were covered with scales. Their skeletons evolved to support longer periods out of the water and their lungs grew more proficient at taking in oxygen. Their eyes, which were once kept moist and clean by the surrounding water, now blinked. A new membrane was developing that would add further protection.

Within the freshwater swamps from which they emerged lurked large pointy-toothed fish that would make an easy meal of them. On land, however, all amphibians had to fear was each other.

As proficient as they became on land, they were still linked to the water when it came time to lay their eggs. As with modern amphibians, their embryos lacked the hard outer shell to protect the eggs throughout development. That protection had to come from the water, and it lasted from the time the eggs were laid to when the larvae developed lungs. (In modern amphibians, many aquatic larvae do not develop lungs. They go from breathing through gills to extracting surface oxygen through their skin.)

The Carboniferous period ushered in a wide variety of tetrapods. Some were little bitty things, like newts. Some looked like great wedge-headed roadkills, with flattened bodies that grew to three feet long. Others resembled Komodo dragons and re-entered the aquatic domain to hunt the shallows, as our alligators do today. And, ironically, after all that work evolution had done to develop legs on fish, the *Orphidepeton*, an ancient legless salamander, went the opposite direction and lost its limbs. We have legless salamanders living today—the Caecilians. They look very much like worms, but they have a spine and hunt food with gaping jaws.

The Labyrinthodonts were most likely at the top of the food chain by the Late Carboniferous period. They ranged in length from a few inches to fifteen feet from head to tail. In appearance, they were newtlike, but unlike our modern newts, these had rows of sharp teeth and, well, could be fifteen feet long. The little ones ate bugs and millipedes and other small creatures; the big ones ate fish and small dinosaurs. They were one of the last surviving large tetrapods. They made it all the way to the Jurassic period, 120 million years ago, and were probably among the last amphibians that could boast that they'd eaten a dinosaur.

With all the vegetation that was now spreading throughout the planet, one might think that amphibians would have been able to take advantage of it as a food source. However, they were, and remain, predators.

•

As seems to be the case throughout the history of life on this planet, the largest of the early amphibians did not make it. They became extinct for a variety of reasons. The smallest animals were the ones that survived to mutate into other life forms. In the middle to Late Carboniferous period, one of these forms, the reptiles, broke the bond of water forever.

A blurry line of distinction separates tetrapods and early reptiles of this time. Many amphibians were reptilelike in appearance and behavior. According to fossil records, a lot of convergent evolution was going on within the vertebrate groups. Fishlike amphibians, amphibianlike amphibians, and reptilelike amphibians all made an appearance. What most likely played a large part in this latter form was amphibians' ability to travel a distance from water. Miles and miles of land must have offered a wealth of food and a haven from predators.

It is true that the reptilelike amphibians were still tied to the water for reproduction, but there must have been occasions when their gelatinous egg masses were laid in water that dried up too soon. A number of amphibians, it is surmised, may have laid their eggs out of the water. Somehow, a few of those embryos had to have made it through that early life cycle to produce new generations of tetrapods that dropped their eggs on land. This could be the group we owe our lives to—those early amphibian/reptile links that upon depositing their eggs on the terra firma thought, *Close enough.*

There are advantages to laying eggs on land. For one, they are easier to hide. Eggs sitting in the shallow water are often highly accessible to the many creatures that eat eggs. Eggs can also wash away in a current. Not having to return to the water to find a mate and lay eggs is also more convenient and draws less attention from predators accustomed to this pattern. Over time, the outer membrane of those eggs grew harder and held moisture long enough for the larvae to develop while still within the egg. Equally important was the addition of the yolk. If the larvae were going to spend some time in the egg, they would need the nourishment that yolks provide. While the adult amphibians still needed water to replenish the body, enough could have easily been found in the form of dew and puddles.

Even today, there are amphibians that lay their eggs out of the water. One of the most common is the redback salamander, which lays its eggs in a damp log. The embryos go through their entire larval stage within their respective eggs and emerge as miniature versions of the adult. So it is not so far-fetched to suggest that this may have been going on during the Carboniferous period.

This changeover from laying eggs in the water to laying them on land could only work if the amphibian was small enough. Larger embryos would need a stronger surrounding structure for support, and this structure would have to hold a proportional amount of water in order for the larval stage to survive. This could explain why the first reptiles started out as very small creatures.

Paleontologists have long sought the missing link between amphibians and reptiles, and they have come close to finding it. One feature that they have determined separates amphibians from reptiles is the otic notch. This is a depression in the back of the skull, in the area where the eardrum was attached, that occurred in amphibians but was missing in early reptiles. That these were lacking in reptiles suggests they were deaf. It is reasonable to assume that as body sizes were shrinking in the earliest reptiles, only the vital features remained intact. Hearing may not have been a vital sense in these rep-phibians and could therefore be sacrificed.

The earliest known reptile, some say, was *Westlothiana lizziae*—nicknamed Lizzie—and it occurred during the Early Carboniferous period. This animal was discovered in Scotland in 1988, and it is believed to be an amniote, or at least amniotelike. An amniote is a creature that comes from an amniotic egg. These eggs have a semipermeable shell that allows oxygen to enter and carbon dioxide to exit, embryonic membranes to enclose the embryo with fluid, a yolk for nutrients, and a cavity for solid wastes. Reptiles lay these kinds of eggs, and so do chickens. Lizzie, the earliest tetrapod exhibiting a wrist and hand that ended in five fingers, is believed to have come from an egg that had some, or all, of these characteristics.

Prior to the discovery of Lizzie, *Hylonomus lyelli* was considered the earliest known reptile, but it actually lived during the Middle Carboniferous period, tens of millions of years after Lizzie. It was found in the mid-1800s by a Nova Scotia–born geologist named Sir William Dawson. Where it was found—in a fossilized hollow stump of a treelike club moss—

is as interesting as its placement among the earliest reptiles. The area of Joggins, Nova Scotia, was once covered with dense stands of great lycopods. Once these trees died, they fell, breaking off at the stump. The trees rotted away, but over time, sediment surrounded the remaining stumps, leaving the middle to rot and collapse. These became pitfall traps for a number of small animals. Dawson's Hylonomus, meaning "forest mouse," was an eight-inch-long lizard that had the misfortune to stumble into a hollow stump.

From there, reptiles went one way and amphibians another. Throughout the Permian period, reptiles began to replace amphibians at the top of the food chain. There were still some formidable salamanders, such as the Labyrinthodonts, to contend with, but their age of dominance was in its twilight. Reptiles grew into quicker and, with a few changes to the musculature of the jaw, better hunters, and they added greens to their menu.

They split into several different groups. One group of reptiles became turtles and tortoises. One group became birds. Another group evolved into mammal-like reptiles, which in turn became mammals. Yet another, the Euryapsids, did very well for themselves for a while: They became dinosaurs (but we already know what happened to them).

Salamanders hold the title of the oldest group of existing terrestrial vertebrates. Unfortunately, there is little fossil evidence to trace their development through the ages. In fact, the attempt to identify the earliest discovered salamander fossil missed by a mile. A Swiss naturalist named Johann Jakob Scheuchzer found it in Germany in 1726. In the early eighteenth century, almost everyone believed the Old Testament to be a historical document (and for many, it still is). Scheuchzer declared that the skeleton he found was, in fact, human remains from Noah's flood. He called it *Homo diluvii testis*, which translates into "head of a flood man." It came to be known as the Diluvian Man, which basically means "flood man." It wasn't until eighty-five years later, in 1811, that the anatomist Georges Cuvier pronounced the remains a giant salamander.

But what about the frogs this whole time? Until now, I have focused on salamanders because frogs came later. We begin to see a hint of them during the Early Triassic period, more than 200 million years ago. The oldest known froglike amphibian was about four inches long and is called *Triadobatrachus*. It looked like a cross between a frog and a salamander, with a little stump of a tail and hind legs a bit longer than the front legs. It could not jump, but would instead have waddled through the swamps and

Triadobatrachus, *an early Triassic frog*

marshes. Interestingly, it looked a lot like a newly metamorphosed froglet.

By the time the age of the dinosaur came about, in the Jurassic period, the frogs we recognize as frogs today were hopping about. The earliest true frog, *Vieraella herbsti*, occurred between 213 and 188 million years ago. It was a little critter, about an inch long, and it contained all the characteristics of a frog—long, powerful hind legs, a short backbone, a fork-shaped hip girdle, and a latticework skull. It also hopped, which was a useful adaptation for dispersal, hunting, and escaping predators. (I can't help but picture one of *Vieraella*'s descendants hopping out from beneath a T-rex's foot seconds before getting crushed.) This hopping ability resulted from the lengthening and strengthening of their hind legs.

In addition to the above, a few other changes were made. The pelvis became elongated and lined up with the spine. The tail receded inside the pelvis and the configuration fused into what is known as a urostyle, which acts as a shock absorber and transfers the force of the legs to the body during a jump. Frogs also developed a movable joint that allows the pelvis to slide up and down the backbone, which helps them to spring into the air.

Since the Jurassic period, frogs have remained relatively unchanged in form. They have survived dinosaurs, meteors, and ice ages. However, with the current decline in frog populations throughout the planet, it seems their biggest challenge for survival lies ahead of them.

While *Vieraella* is known from the oldest of the modern amphibian fossils, it still followed the salamanders. The oldest Caudata fossils were recently found in northern China. About 161 million years ago, a volcano erupted and buried many thousands of salamanders. Adults and larvae were preserved by this event, and some were so well preserved it was possible to see their eyes, internal gills and, within their stomachs, their last meal of clam shrimp. The species, which resembled today's hellbenders, were named *Chunerpeton tianyiensis*.

Before the discovery of *Chunerpeton*, the former Soviet Union claimed the title of being home to the oldest Caudata fossil. Named *Karaurus sharovi*, this organism was a little over half a foot long and dragged itself about through the Jurassic period, roughly 140 million years ago. Like *Chunerpeton*, this was a fully specialized salamander, which strongly suggests a lineage that began long before the appearance of this individual, and that of frogs. Frog and salamander remains do not weather the ages very well; their delicate bones make poor candidates for fossilization.

One thing we can determine from the fossils that have been found is that the salamanders did most of their evolving in North America, specifically in the Northeast. They spread out from there to Asia, Europe, and the far northern reaches of Africa before the continents began to drift apart. Still, North America held on to all but two species of the Plethodons (lungless salamanders). Frog fossils, however, are found on every continent, including Antarctica. In fact, they had already arrived in Europe and Africa by the Late Jurassic period. It's fun to imagine that their ability to jump great distances had something to do with their wide distribution, and that may just be the case. For every step a salamander takes, a similarly sized frog can more than quadruple the distance.

It took frogs and salamanders many leaps and steps to get to where they are today, as it did *Homo sapiens*. What if those early tetrapods had never left the water? Or had left it, hated it, and jumped back in? Evolution might never have found us. What about those opposable thumbs we so cherish and laud? Chances are a need would never have arisen for them to develop. We probably wouldn't have to worry about things like air pollution or internal combustion engines or even the hiccups.

Good or bad, frogs and salamanders did invade the land. Those which survived created new generations that either adapted or perished. We are the product of the adapters. And as different as we appear from those Carboniferous and Devonian creatures, we share with them their love of the water. How many of us don't enjoy a good soak in a pool now and then? Just try and get kids to come out of the water before their fingers and toes get all pruney. We love the water! We love to look at it, swim through it, float on it, and live next to it. Within our homes are large basins we fill with it in which to immerse ourselves.

And then there are those hands. While we took a different fork in the road about 300 million years ago, we and frogs and salamanders managed to hold on to those fingers and palms our ancestors seemed to have gotten correct at the outset.

❧ 3 ❧

Salamander Rain

It's been raining all day, and it's the first good rain since the onset of winter. The frozen March ground ponds the water in a wide sheet across the yard. Gritty cores of plow- and shovel-built piles are all that's left of the snow. The temperature has been above 40 degrees the last few days and the snowmelt is being drawn to the vernal pool basins throughout the lower Northeast. This rain will top it off nicely. The meteorologists are unanimous in their call for pouring rain well into the next morning. (As is custom with the media, they are working themselves into a frenzy over this pending rainstorm. The weather anchors have been at it day and night, their voices now hoarse, and in apologetic tones, they share the ill tidings along with a healthy dose of vital rainy weather tips we viewers need to survive this event. In a way, I suppose, they are heroes.)

I'm excited. I've been waiting for the rain—specifically one that begins in the afternoon and goes on into the night. I prepared for this night about a week ago: I checked the batteries in the flashlights and made sure I had film in the camera; I placed my boots, raincoat, chest waders (just in case), hat, and gloves in a corner; and I packed various jars and nets and pans in the wet bag.

Other people are getting antsy, too. The phone has been ringing and e-mails have been coming and going since last night. "You think this one is it?" is the question. I do.

EVERY YEAR, I await the salamander rain. It is a phenomenon that happens throughout the Northeast in the months of March and April and earlier in the south. Many of us look forward to this event year after year. During the first warm late winter/early spring rain, one that begins at least by late afternoon and continues into the night, mole salamanders leave their underground burrows by the millions to seek out vernal pools in which to breed. So too, do the wood frogs. Either or both can be found just about everywhere the proper habitat, vernal pools surrounded by deciduous woods, exists. Quite often, roads bisect these vernal pools and

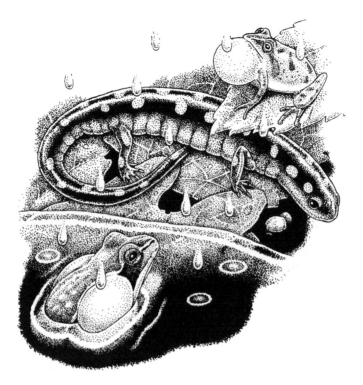

The amphibian trinity: wood frog, spring peeper, and spotted salamander

woodlands, which makes access far easier and more convenient. On the down side, a lot of amphibian carnage is left behind.

Vernal pools are meccas to a handful of amphibians in our area. Five species are dependent on them—spotted, Jefferson, and marbled salamanders, wood frogs, and spadefoot toads. Blue-spotted salamanders will also use these vernal pools, as will other species of frogs and salamanders that can afford to be more cosmopolitan. This habitat is defined by varying criteria, but it is most universally accepted that a vernal pool is a basin with no permanent outlet (basically, self contained), and that it is dry for a part of the year. Any frog or salamander that lays its eggs in one of these bodies of water benefits by not having its offspring eaten by fish, which can go through a mass of frog eggs in no time.

For these habitats to support amphibian life, they need to be surrounded by trees. Not only do the trees regulate the temperature (shade) and level of the water (osmosis), but upland, their dead leaves offer shelter

Giant Water Bugs

The giant water bug is a true bug in the Hemiptera family. While water bugs resemble beetles, they are distinguished in part by how they feed. Most Hemiptera have sucking mouthparts, and many feed by piercing the skin with a sharp beak and then drinking the contents. The giant water bug pierces all kinds of things. Its shield-shaped body is a uniform deep burnt umber. Two black beads for eyes protrude from the mostly hidden head. It has a Darth Vader look to it. It floats at the surface of the water breathing from a snorkel that protrudes from the tip of its abdomen. (Yes, it's an ass-breather.) When a little fish, tadpole, bug, or young salamander swims too close, the giant water bug lunges with a kick of its paddle feet, grabs its prey with its front claws, inserts its beak, and drinks its meal like a milkshake. The fact that these bugs can be as big as two and a half inches long gives them some clout.

Incidentally, you don't want to get bitten by one of these. It's been said that you either experience extreme pain, then numbness, then pain or numbness, then extreme pain, then more pain. Whichever the order, you will feel both extreme pain and numbness. However, giant water bugs are delicious to eat, and are considered a delicacy in some parts of the world. (I ate one once—cooked, of course. I found it to be quite tasty, with a somewhat salty banana flavor.)

The giant water bug, a.k.a. Eastern toe-biter

to the dispersed animals. In the vernal pools themselves, are the ingredients that kick off the food chain. Various bacteria and arthropods eat the decaying leaves, which are eaten by other organisms, which, in turn, are eaten by larger ones. This continues up to the top of the food chain ladder where the amphibians are perched. Here is a place where a little, rubbery, bug-eyed insectivore can rule the domain. Having survived the many insect perils—dragonfly nymphs, water beetles, and water scorpions—in their tadpole and larval stage, they emerge as the big frogs in the little pond. Their closest competitor is still an insect—the giant water bug, aka the Eastern toe biter.

Many of these insects are making the migration to these pools as well, but generally not in the rain. Some have overwintered as eggs, laid the previous summer. The fairy shrimp, which are crustaceans, also spend the winter in this state. Once the late-winter flooding has filled their pools, they emerge to dance in the sunlight streaming through the tree branches. Their dance is actually feeding activity. They are filter feeders, sliding upside down through the water, taking in plankton, bacteria, and organic matter. Some seasons come and go without the appearance of fairy shrimp because their eggs can go several years without hatching. This allows them to survive the marginal pools that don't stay filled as long or as frequently. You can check the same pool year after year and see nothing, only to discover an explosion of fairy shrimp the following year. They go through several life cycles before the pool has emptied, and the last generation of the year lays eggs that must dry out before hatching. These truly ephemeral creatures have evolved to take advantage of the uncertain patterns of a habitat that is sometimes there and sometimes not.

Fairy shrimp

While it is always a treat to find fairy shrimp in the newly filled pool, it still doesn't beat putting yourself in the middle of the amphibian migration. In the area where I live, I consider this the second considerable migration of a new year. In February, the amphibians are preceded by the red-winged blackbirds. Hearing that unmistakable "Kee-ooo-reeee" coming from the marshes is the first sign that winter is coming to an end. We notice these things in the Northeast. This time of year, we've gotten about everything we could out of winter and are ready to move on. Come the middle to the end of winter, we look for signs of spring wherever we can find them. And a few are around by late February to mid-March. The skunk cabbage has pushed its rolled shoots up through the ice. Pussy willows are in full bud. Moths are appearing at my porch light—sallows, quakers, and pinions, mostly, and the occasional Bruce spanworm. Stoneflies are bouncing over the open water in streams and ponds. Great horned owls are about finished incubating their eggs, and soon, we can expect to hear that pleasantly grating call of the young screaming for food.

The migration of the frogs and salamanders is the biggie, though. Its significance won't be matched until, perhaps, the arrival of the first butterflies, which are usually Mourning Cloaks in late March. Then, the warbler migration comes in May. Of course, there is the earthworm migration, consisting of only a few feet, straight up. Earthworms journey toward the ground's surface as it thaws. This is a massive migration, possibly the largest of all the creatures in the area, but since it takes place below our feet, it goes unnoticed.

The spring amphibian migration is not significant because of the distances they travel. At the upper end of their journey, they cover a little over a thousand feet. What makes it such a phenomenal event to me is that we get to see these generally secretive creatures out in the open, and in huge numbers. It's an event that has taken place for thousands of years because it is an act that ensures reproduction and, therefore, survival.

The key players in this phenomenon are the spotted, blue-spotted, and Jefferson salamanders, and the wood frogs. All waited out the winter in underground burrows, of another creature's making, beneath the woodland duff. The salamanders were in a state of semihibernation while the wood frogs were actually frozen solid. Salamanders do not have the ability to survive freezing, so they winter below the frost line. The warmer nights and heavy rains wake them from their slumber, and they work their way to the surface, often pushing through snow to get there. Then it is a crawl and a hop to the nearby vernal pools.

The pools are like singles' clubs for the amphibian set. The males generally arrive first, sometimes by a few days, or even weeks, and they wait for the females to arrive. As soon as the females enter the clear pools, they are inundated with male suitors. I have seen huge masses of spotted salamanders, called a congress, about thirty strong, formed by males trying to get the attention of a single female. There are times when the water is churning with congresses throughout the pool. Meanwhile, the smaller male wood frogs are piling on the gravid females.

The frogs and salamanders can also have a different, less amorous, greeting party waiting for them. I saw one pool with a line of leeches stretched out along the edge. These were *Macrobdella*, or freshwater leeches, which can grow to about ten inches long. They are the same leeches used to prevent clotting in reattachment surgery. While they feed on a variety of vertebrates, including humans, they have a real appetite for frog eggs, as well as the frogs themselves. A study at the University of Michigan tested whether it was movement or scent that triggers this species' feeding behavior. A sheepskin condom was filled with blood and lowered among the leeches in the water. They took no interest. Then a frog was rubbed on the condom, it was put back in the water, and the leeches proceeded to go into a feeding frenzy. Imagine what it must be like to not just smell like a frog but actually be one. The leeches I saw at the edge of the pool were waiting in whatever passes for leech anticipation as their unknowing amphibian hosts entered the water to offer sustenance. It was disconcerting, but even leeches have some aesthetic value. When their rotaries of teeth are not clamped onto flesh, pumping in leech saliva and pumping out blood, they glide over the leaves like graceful, undulating ribbons. Their undersides are a cheerfully bright salmon color while above is deep olive green lined with rows of bright red spots. If you can get beyond their appetite for blood, they're not so bad. Really.

The night, however, does not belong exclusively to wood frogs, mole salamanders, and leeches. Spring peepers also emerge to make their way to pools and more permanent bodies of water. They, too, can freeze solid and, at times, they wake up too soon for their own good. On more than one occasion, I've heard a lone peeper peeping over a snow-covered landscape in December or January or February, awakened too soon by a warm winter sun. Any of these early season amphibians can jump the gun. (A friend of mine just sent me a photo he took of a spotted salamander while he was cross-country skiing on Groundhog's Day. What happens when a salamander sees its shadow on the second of February remains to be seen.)

Four-toed and redback salamanders cross the wet roads, too. They do not use vernal pools to breed, but the water on the road makes traveling ideal for those with bodies that need to stay damp. Another mole salamander, the marbled salamander, can also be found crossing this time of year. Their breeding took place the previous fall, so for them, too, the rain is more of a vehicle for dispersal.

The first time I witnessed this migration was with Kay and Hank Kudlinski. Kay is a naturalist, writer, and illustrator who does a weekly column, "The Naturalist," for the New Haven Register *in Connecticut. Hank, her husband, is a world traveling, scuba diving, black-belt metals salesman. Kay had written one of her weekly articles about the salamander migration. At the time, I had never even heard of this phenomenon, and her article made me eager to catch it underway. Kay offered to take me to a good spot by her house some rainy night, and to expect a phone call when the time was right, which could be as late as 10:30.*

The phone call came about 9:00 p.m. a few nights later. Betsy, my kids, Jeff and Liz, and I piled into the car and drove a couple towns over. We met up with Kay and Hank, who were standing alongside the road searching the ground with flashlights. I saw something moving in the light of Hank's flashlight; it was my first spotted salamander sighting. I wondered how I could have missed these creatures all my life. They are so big, and with those yellow spots, quite noticeable, and they look so primordial.

This one had stopped moving, apparently assessing potential danger from the six humans around it. Its belly hugged the cold ground, but that tadpole-shaped head was held high. It was the position of someone who can't get the back half of his or her body off the floor to complete a push-up. The eyes were shiny black beads that reflected Hank's flashlight. I wondered how closely those eyes resembled the eyes of our early terrestrial ancestors millenniums ago. They were cold, but not lifeless, and aware, but not overtly curious. How much detail surrounds the basic information it takes in? Can it experience a form of amphibian fear or contentment? Was it smelling us as well as looking at us?

In short time, I realized salamanders were all over the road, which raised a new question: How many did I run over on the way here? The road bisects the upland woods, from where they were migrating, and the vernal pool, where they were heading.

*In the water, the sala-
manders became different
creatures entirely. They
were transformed from
awkward body draggers to
wriggly aquatics, scooting
through the water. When
they walked, it appeared as
if they were weightless,
bouncing like moon walkers
across the leafy bottom.*

What do those eyes see?

*Ever-present was the
chortling of wood frogs.
They floated in a big circle
along the surface, arms and
legs akimbo. Their throats bubbled out on the sides as they claimed territories and
called for companionship. At times, two would leave the circle and charge each
other. From my vantage point, not much seemed to happen when they met. They
just stopped and swam back to where they had been.*

*They were all over the road, too, and while the spotted salamanders brought
to mind the word* primitive, *the wood frogs took me in a different direction. I
picked one up and looked right into that masked face. Frogs look cool. By cool, I
mean unassuming "Let it happen. I can't be bothered, man" cool. If spotted salamanders are pleiocene relics, wood frogs are 1950s beatniks.*

*Scattered among the bare branches surrounding the pools were chorusing
spring peepers. Each peep from what had to be fifty to one hundred individual
peepers, maybe more, blended into a trembly, high-pitched peal. At some points,
they were so loud and so close, my eardrums would crackle and buzz. As loud as
their calls are, though, seeing one of these little frogs can be a challenge. They
tend to stop calling if you shine a light on them. These really are tiny and their
cryptic coloration makes them look like the surrounding dead leaves. They can be
found, though, with triangulation. It helps to cup your ears to home in on a single
individual. Once you think you have found the source of your call, you shine your
light in that area. If the peeping stops, you are probably looking right at it. Be
patient, wait a few moments, and the peeping will most likely resume. It is
amazing how far the throat bubbles out—about two-thirds the size of the body.*

That first "salameander" I observed with the Kudlinskis set my life on a
whole new course. At least the part of my life that I live in March and

April. Not a spring season has gone by since that I have not spent many
cold rainy nights seeking out these amphibians. I love doing this. Not only
is there something to be said for squeezing pleasure and excitement from
the most miserable weather, but seeing my first frogs and salamanders of
the year is like greeting old friends.

And then there are the following mornings, when a search along the
edges of the pools will reveal the fruit of their loins and labors. The spring-
breeding mole salamanders, and the wood frogs, leave behind gelatinous
masses of eggs, ranging in size from a small sausage to a softball, depending on the breed and an individual's egg-producing prowess. The eggs
of the spotted salamander and wood frog look similar. The best way to tell
the difference is by the shape of the outer surface. In a wood frog egg mass,
you can see the outline of each individual globule surrounding the embryo;
in the spotted salamander egg mass, the outer surface lacks those rounded
bumps. As the season progresses, the wood frog's egg mass breaks up and
floats along the surface, allowing the individual embryos to absorb more
heat from the sun. It also collects symbiotic algae. The egg mass of the
salamander remains relatively intact and retains its clear or cloudy white
color, although it, too, can become infused with some algae.

At first, I was alone on these nightly jaunts. I would drive about in the
rain, looking for likely spots, or better yet, crossing salamanders. Then I'd
fasten up the rain gear and walk up and down the road, sweeping my flashlight back and forth. This activity often takes place in neighborhoods, and
it is not unusual to have someone call the cops on me. It's understandable,
really. It's 11 p.m., and you peek out your window to see some guy walking
back and forth on your street, looking for who knows what with his flashlight. So far, it has been pretty easy to convince the police as to why I'm
out there. Usually, the frogs and salamanders can back up my claims.

Being out on such a night *is* a different experience, and the two down
sides can be easily overcome. It is cold, so you wear warm clothes, and it
is wet, so you cover those clothes with a raincoat and rain pants. We are
habituated to do anything we can to avoid putting ourselves in these conditions, but once the problem of the cold and wet is solved, a serenity and
a sense of isolation takes hold. This is a new niche to explore. It exists only
at night; its borders are marked by season, temperature, and rainfall. It is
a time and place where things are awakening and breeding, a culmination
of purpose for these creatures. To see these things you have to put yourself there. It's almost like visiting a different part of the country, and it's

unfamiliar, even when it is a place you have been to many times in the daylight. The air has that somewhat fishy smell of a neglected aquarium. I always associate that smell with salamanders, although I believe it actually emanates from the rotting leaves.

While wood frogs, spring peepers, and spotted salamanders make up the bulk of the herpetological biota on these nights, many other amphibians are on the move as well, such as pickerel, green, and bull frogs, red-spotted newts, two-lined, four-toed, and redback salamanders, and American and spadefoot toads. Many of them are emaciated from not eating for almost half a year. The roads are lined with worms washed from their tunnels. These would seem an easy treat for these famished frogs and salamanders, but not necessarily so. They cannot eat until their digestive systems have warmed up, which takes a bit longer to activate than their mechanical abilities. What a waste of good worms, although, I suppose, some are gobbled up by those that have had longer to thaw.

People driving by often roll down their windows to ask me if I need help. I always welcome these opportunities to tell them and show them, if possible, what I'm doing. Most have never seen a spotted salamander before, let alone realize how many they have been flattening with their cars. I now have signs, made by local herpetologist Chuck Landry, that I can put up when I prepare to search a road. It reads, "Raining Tonight? Salamanders Crossing! Please Slow Down Next____Feet." Granted, not everyone's going to slow down, but I imagine this arouses the curiosity of a number of people enough to check to see if the warning is real. At the very least, it would explain why that guy is out in the road in the middle of the night in the pouring rain. (I know a couple of people who keep the signs up even when they are not there, but some of these signs have been stolen.)

Vehicular amphibicide *is* a real problem, though. Frogs and salamanders are not savvy when it comes to road

If you spot one of these by the roadside on a rainy spring night, slow down and watch carefully for migrating amphibians and a lurking herpetologist.

crossing. One of the ways I discover new locations is by finding the DORs (Dead On Road) as I drive about. The insides of frogs and salamanders stand out better against the black asphalt than their outsides do. Where there are DORs, there are sure to be living counterparts. While the amphibian populations can take a hit by vehicular traffic, and have for decades, at some point, increased losses can severely diminish or wipe out that population. I have witnessed populations decrease as surrounding development increases—more houses mean more cars on the road. Such is the fate of wood frogs and spotted salamanders at one of my earlier spots. There, they have to cross a fairly busy town road. That road has grown exponentially busier since it has become the route to a set of outlet stores one town over. I have watched what was once a thriving population sink down to just a handful crossing. Chances are against them rebounding; in general, the nature of traffic is that it gets worse, not better.

When I am on a road and a car is coming, I will pick up a frog or salamander that is in danger and carry it over to the other side. In a season, I will have done this with roughly fifty to a hundred individuals. Will this protect their populations? In the big picture, it probably won't make much difference at all, but that's not why I do it. I do it for the individual salamander whose life I've extended for at least one part of its journey—it does have to make it back to the woods after breeding in the pool. These amphibians live for a handful of years, and it seems unjust that they survive all the trials of the wild only to have their lives end beneath a car tire. I also feel good knowing that I may have helped a salamander or frog bring dozens more into the world.

Something else is happening that may make more of a difference. Over the years, I have been running into more and more people out in the salamander rain. This kind of outing is growing in popularity, and people I would never have expected to see out in these miserable conditions are as hooked on this as I am. Not one of them can pass up the opportunity to play crossing guard. If you have dozens of people rescuing hundreds of amphibians, it can't hurt. There is also the education element, because there are more of us out there explaining to the passing drivers that it is possible to drive without running them over. It just takes a bit longer. It is always satisfying to watch these drivers taking their time after our encounter.

●

John Ogren has started something interesting with Boy Scout Troop 51 in the town of Old Saybrook, Connecticut. He wanted to show his scouts the salamander migration and with my help found a good reliable spot. He and the kids spent the night crossing more than 240 salamanders. It was such a success that the following year the troop turned it into a fund-raiser. People were invited to pledge a certain amount of money for each salamander escorted safely to its destination. The money raised would be used to help fund a trip to Glacier National Park, in Montana, where the scouts were going to plant trees. I found it pleasing to think about how one good deed could be used to fund another. In addition to raising $1,500 for rescuing more than 450 salamanders, the activity also went toward earning a merit badge. What an incredible idea. With all the scout troops out there, boy and girl, this is something that could have a great impact on some of the local amphibian populations.

I joined John and the troop in 2005. While they did not take pledges that year, the dozen scouts and family members showed no less enthusiasm. In fact, it became a competition to see who could save the most. This became apparent even in the youngest of volunteers, eight-year-old Maizie Ogren, whose brother, Anders, is a scout in the troop.

"I only got six," she said.

"That's good," said John, her dad.

Maizie was not convinced. Then she shouted, "Dad, stop!" John was only inches away from stepping on a spotted salamander. Maizie scooped it up and carried it to the edge of the road where it was headed. "You almost stepped on it," she said.

"Nice save. That should count as three more," I said.

"Seven," said Maizie.

When I walked up the road a bit, I overheard two of the scouts comparing numbers. One was up to thirty-two, and the other thought he was at twenty-eight. When I asked who had the most in the troop

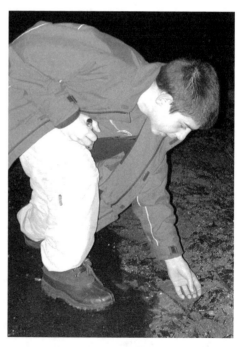

Boy Scout Patrick Malin rescuing a spotted salamander.

so far, they named one of the boys and said, with obvious admiration, that he was up to forty-four.

Other groups out there aid these creatures as well. Many are doing volunteer work for their statewide amphibian monitoring projects. They are listening to frog calls, counting migrants, checking under rocks and logs in their cover searches, and recording all that they find. This information goes to a central database where biologists attempt to assess the state of the amphibian in their respective areas. (This is discussed more in the chapter on conservation titled "Save the Salamanders!")

I am signed onto a vernal pool listserve, which is fairly quiet most of the year, but come salamander season it explodes with activity, mimicking the explosion in the amphibian activity we are all so interested in. People from Maine to Virginia are not only posting their findings, but discussing amphibian conservation issues, where to find what, and helping each other with all manner of questions regarding amphibians, fairy shrimp, and their habitats. It has become quite a phenomenon in itself, and one can almost watch the warmer weather creep its way up north by the reports of the first frog and salamander sightings. For example, someone in Long Island, New York, will be reporting egg masses, and maybe even tadpoles, weeks before Mainers have heard a peep over their frozen ponds. Once we get our first Maine reports, those south of them can be assured that spring has settled in the Northeast. (The listserve was developed by Matthew Burne, and you can find more information about it at http://groups.yahoo.com/group/vernalpool.) Most of the people on this list can boast of having helped many amphibians across the road.

●

Frogs and salamanders are cold to the touch, at least this time of year. Some can be quite sluggish, having just awakened, while others are alert and active. Regardless, the last thing you want to do is drop them, especially salamanders, because they are not designed to land on their feet—or to land, period. They evolved as ground-hugging creatures with no adaptations for what follows having been airborne. Frogs have only a slightly better chance surviving a crash landing on asphalt from the height of a standing human. For this reason, when taxiing amphibians across a road, one should hold them as close to the ground as possible in case they wriggle free.

Mole salamanders can exude a sticky substance when threatened. It is a deterrent to predators but is not harmful to humans unless they were to eat one, or put any part of their hand that has handled a salamander in their mouth. They will live, but the bitter taste will negate any plans they may have had to test the flavor of another.

That unpleasant taste only occurs on the outer skin of the amphibian. While few creatures will eat a live mole salamander, they have no problem with the DORs. A road littered with the bodies of dead frogs and salamanders will be virtually picked clean by crows, raccoons, and skunks in no time.

A normal person does not find the feel of a cold, wet, sticky amphibian a pleasurable one. One friend would carry a packet of tissues with her for that reason. As much as she didn't like picking them up, it was important enough to her to save some lives, so she found a way. It's also a great way to prevent spreading pathogens or fungi or any undesirable conditions from one amphibian to another. I usually wear a pair of cotton work gloves, not so much because I mind the feel of the amphibian, but it makes them less slippery and keeps my hands warmer.

One important rule to follow when helping amphibians cross is to know where they are going. On the first few rainy nights it's easy, because they are all going to the ponds. You will see very few frogs and salamanders crossing in different directions. In the rains that follow, though, there will be a reverse migration back to the woods. This is a more piecemeal occurrence, staggered over a longer period of time, and there may be some latecomers, too, still heading to the water. Depositing your amphibian on the wrong side of the road will force it to cross again. And every crossing is a life or death gamble.

A spotted salamander risks a road crossing.

After a few years of seeking out spotted salamanders and wood frogs, I grew anxious to see some of the other salamanders that migrated on these nights. I had never seen a blue-spotted or Jefferson salamander because they are not in my area. They both migrate in the same manner; the only difference is that the blue-spotted salamanders are not restricted to vernal pools. They also use red maple swamps. Both of these species are state listed in Connecticut; the blue-spotted is listed as Threatened and the Jefferson is listed as Special Concern. Habitat loss and traffic are to be blamed for their decreased numbers.

I got a tip on a blue-spotted location that was, to my surprise, only about twenty minutes from my home. So there I was one rainy night, walking up and down the long road, my flashlight sweeping back and forth. On one side of the road was a very large red maple swamp. It sat at the base of a small mountain that was being disassembled for gravel. On the other side of the road were houses. While I am sure many of the salamanders I was looking for would be entering the water from the mountain side, it was my hope that the homeowners on the other side had left enough trees to harbor these creatures for the rest of the year. If so, those creatures would have to cross the road to get to the water.

I was looking for something I'd never laid my eyes on, which is different from looking for something you have actually seen. Sure, I've looked at pictures of this amphibian, but it's hard to get a true sense of the size until you've seen it in the wild. After about two hours of searching this road, I gave up. I had found many spotted salamanders, wood frogs, and peepers, which were nice to see, but they were not my quarry. The next rains came a few days later and I returned to this spot again. One hour, two hours, and still nothing sighted. The rain was beginning to let up, and when this happens, there is a break in the activity. The more it rains, the more they move. I walked back to my car, which was parked at the very end of the road by a streetlight. I had passed the main part of the swamp and began to ease up in my search. That's when I saw something wriggling across the road under the light. I figured it was another spotted salamander, and when I got closer, I gave it a shot with the beam of my flashlight. It wasn't a spotted salamander; it was too small, and more important, it didn't have yellow spots. It did have little blue spots, though. It had stopped walking and turned its head toward the light. I was looking at a blue-spotted salamander and I remember the exact words that came out of my mouth: "Holy crap!"

It is hard to describe the excitement that washed over me. It came from setting out to find something rare and actually finding it. Persistence was involved, but so was luck. If I had been a minute later or sooner, I would have missed it, and it was such a beautiful creature. It appeared a bit more delicate in stature than the spotted salamanders, and the blue flecking over its body brought to mind old enamelware pans. The tail was slightly keeled, and when I went to pick the animal up, it raised its tail off the ground, holding it in a shallow arc. I wondered if this action is to entice a predator to go for that instead of the more important parts. Giving up the tail in exchange for escape is something that some salamanders do.

Seconds after coming upon this creature, I was struck by the fact that I was alone. I was bursting to share this with my friends, but it was about one in the morning, and they were most likely in bed or out hunting their own amphibians. I scooped it up and put it in my pocket until I got to the car. Grabbing a jar from my wet bag (the bag I take out on these nights), I filled it with wet leaves and added the salamander. I wanted to photograph it in the daylight the next morning, but, more important, I wanted my friends to have the opportunity to see it. Like me, none of them had seen a blue-spotted salamander before.

I left the jar outside overnight so the salamander wouldn't be subjected to a dramatic temperature change. After a bunch of phone calls, six people joined me the following afternoon back at the site where it was found. It was important to me that it be returned to its habitat as soon as possible. (When I do bring one of these amphibians home, I make a point to get it back the very next day.)

We all gathered around the blue-spotted salamander, marveling and photographing. Then I picked it up and carried it over to the water where it was headed fifteen hours before and set it on the edge. It immediately shot into the water, where it swam like no spotted salamander I'd ever seen. It was that keeled tail. I suppose that a creature in a larger habitat, like a swamp, needs better swimming skills than one that only navigates in a vernal pool. This critter blended in so well with the underwater backdrop, it disappeared in a quick moment.

I visit this site every year now. Some years I find blue-spotted salamanders, and some years I don't. It wasn't until I found a full adult that I realized the first one had not been fully grown.

•

Having found the blue-spotted, only one more remained on my hit list—

the Jefferson salamander. Again, I had a tip on where to find one. This came from Hank Gruner, a herpetologist who is with the Science Center of Connecticut. He told me of a vernal pool in Hartford County that contains Jeffersons, which have been confirmed as two-thirds *jeffersonianum*. Many of the Jeffersons and blue-spotteds in Connecticut have interbred throughout history, so finding a pure population of either, while they exist, is more difficult.

This particular area was a bit over an hour from my house, but it sounded like a sure thing. The month was April, but this year had been a particularly cold one and snow still lingered in parts of the state from a hard winter. When the first warmish rain finally arrived, it poured. It started in early evening, which was a little too late to bring anything out from the ground, at least by a respectable hour. But I had to try, so I set out around 10 p.m. to give the rain more of a chance to do its work. Finding the vernal pool was fairly easy, but what I had not counted on was the snow. Because I was an hour inland from my home, the temperature was colder. What was rain at home was snow and sleet up here, which was not conducive to finding amphibians.

But I was here and decided to give it a go anyway. The pool was off the road by about 100 feet and was surrounded by homes on three sides and woods on one. It was too miserable a night for people to be out and about, so I had the road to myself. I walked from one end to the other, about a quarter of a mile each way, in a slow serpentine pattern, trying to cover as much of the road as possible. Absolutely nothing was out. No wood frogs called in the distance. No peepers, no spotted salamanders, not even any washed-out worms. Somehow the sleet had found a way down the back of my coat. While it was an unpleasant sensation, it did keep me awake. I had forgotten my gloves, which was a big mistake, especially since my flashlight was metal. As time went by, I shifted the light between my numbing hands more and more frequently. Because I knew I had a warm car waiting, the discomfort was bearable.

I looked at my watch. It was quarter after twelve and time to call it quits. I had walked way past my car and slowly made my way back, still searching, but knowing that this was a complete waste of time. I slipped off my wet gear, crawled in the car, and cranked the heat. The windows immediately fogged up and it would be a few minutes before I could hit the road. As the car warmed, I thought about the nice dry bed waiting for me. I wouldn't be getting home until well after one in the morning. Drives back from these outings are always more enjoyable when I have something to show for my efforts. This time would be less pleasant. On a positive note, while I'd failed to turn up my Jefferson salamander, I now knew where to look and could return on another night.

When the windows finally cleared, I turned on the headlights to begin the trip home. The mixture of rain, snow, and sleet had coated the road with a clear frosting. I'd rolled about forty feet when I saw a salamander in the road in front of me. It was practically swimming through the sleet, moving and pausing, moving and pausing. I stepped on the brakes and slid a couple feet closer the amphibian. "No!" I shouted. The car stopped just short of running it over, and I flew out the door. The salamander was frozen in the headlights. It was about five or six inches from head to tail, uniformly colored a deep slate gray, and it had no yellow spots. It was a Jefferson. "Oh my God," I said. "Oh my God."

The Jefferson salamander is not the most striking creature on earth, but I could not have enjoyed looking at it more had it been sporting multicolored glow-in-the-dark antennae. A large part of its allure lay in having never seen one before, being able to find it, and knowing what it goes through every spring. There is also something to be said for seeing a creature that has so few defenses out in the open. Granted, it is night, and its largest threat comes by way of traffic, but this is the one time in its life where it is out from under cover. This is the big, and essential, gamble it

A Jefferson salamander in the snow

must take to complete the life cycle. Again, the questions come. Does it sense the danger it is in at this point? It must, because there seems an urgency to get to where it is going. It will not linger any longer than it takes to get its bearings. What manner of threat do I pose? My eyes are located on the front of my face for binocular vision, a position many animals recognize as a predator trait. I want to assure this creature that I mean it no harm.

I looked at the side of the road from where it had come. The entire area was under six inches of snow. Once it crossed the road, it would have to travel through even more snow all the way to the vernal pool, which was covered with ice. This salamander had climbed out of the frozen ground, through half a foot of snow, to then be pelted by sleet. It would drag its belly through the snow again to find a way under the layer of ice into what would comparably be a cozy pool of water. And it would accomplish all this with a body about as naked as a body can be—no fur, feathers, or scales for protection.

I'm not sure I should have done what I did next, but I went back to the car, found a jar, and brought the salamander home. Again, I knew there would be some people interested in seeing it. The only caveat would be that they would have to come first thing in the morning, because I was anxious to return the salamander as soon as possible. In truth, I don't think one night missed in the pond would have made much difference anyway. I doubt there would be many, if any, salamander mates there.

The only one who could make it was a friend, Carol Lemmon. Before her recent retirement, Carol was the deputy State Entomologist with the Connecticut Agricultural Experiment Center. She also loves amphibians and had never seen a Jefferson salamander. She joined me on the ride back to Hartford County. It was still raining as we sloshed through the wet snow to the edge of the pool and set the Jefferson salamander down. It slid across the surface and slipped under the ice. It was truly a satisfying moment.

A Light at the End of the Tunnel

A couple hundred people gathered on a drizzly rainy evening along the length of Henry Street in Amherst, Massachusetts. The crowd was made up of media, scientists, amphibian well-wishers, and curiosity seekers of all ages. There were so many people that the road was closed for their safety. It was March 1988, and they were there to watch the salamanders cross beneath the road via two tunnels constructed the previous fall for just this purpose. The project was over-seen by herpetologist Tom Tyning, and it was the first of its kind attempted in North America.

The weather reports were promising for that evening; rain beginning ear-lier in the day was expected to go well into the night. It was sprinkling around 6:30 p.m. By 7:00 p.m., it stopped, and the salamanders, which need rain to fa-cilitate their migration, slept in. People were growing impatient as the minutes crawled by. Then someone found a male spotted salamander farther up the hill. He brought it down to the tunnel to see what it would do. Hit by so many flash-light beams, the salamander turned around and headed back to the woods.

Eventually, the people went home, disappointed.

About 10:30 that evening, the rain returned, and Tom headed back to the site

Tom Tyning 'phibing

to check on the tunnels. He didn't know if the salamanders would use the tunnel to cross the road, or if they would allow themselves to be corralled to the tunnels' entrance by drift fences. It was possible that when the salamanders encountered the fences, they would turn around. The rain brought the salamanders; they filed along the drift fences to the mouth of the tunnels. While some showed hesitation, most entered the tunnels and emerged safely on the other side. It was a success. The media were alerted and news of the Amherst tunnels spread far and wide.

According to Mr. Tyning, his boss handed this project to him while he was with Massachusetts Audubon. The British Flora and Fauna Preservation Society, who wished to see their concept of toad tunnels expanded to other parts of the world, had contacted Mr. Tyning's boss. With help from the British society and other local groups, the two tunnels were constructed beneath the two-lane road in the fall of 1986. The Amherst Department of Public Works provided the labor, many of whom had no idea what a spotted salamander even looked like. A few who did, knew them only as fish bait. Their main concern was safety issues with the road, the surface of which would be bisected by a grate to allow light and moisture within the tunnel. The tunnel material, donated by ACO Polymer Products Ltd. of Germany, was plasticized concrete, because plain concrete absorbs moisture and is not a surface friendly to amphibian physiology.

Mr. Tyning, who is currently Professor of Environmental Science at Berkshire, says the tunnels continue to provide safe access for the migrating amphibians nearly twenty years after their installation. They are self-sustaining and have held up well to traffic, both above and below. Observers have learned over time that ponded water at the entrance and exit of the tunnel and light shined at the end help encourage the movement of the salamanders.

The United States has close to four million miles of roads. While they are necessary to allow us to get to where we are going, they do pose a huge problem for wildlife. Not only do the roads themselves fragment wildlife habitat and facilitate pollution runoff, the vehicles that traverse them are responsible for a staggering number of wildlife mortalities. According to Defenders of Wildlife: "As cities large and small grow, the associated spider-like road network means that the places wildlife go for food and water—forests and streams—also undergo fundamental change. The bottom line is that altering their habitat has resulted in more than one million animals killed on our highways every day. In fact, road kill is the number one way that humans kill wildlife in the United States." They urge people to get involved in road planning in their area.

We do need to keep highways far from sensitive areas and make existing roads more compatible with wildlife. Naturally, this begins with identifying which lands are important to the long-term survival of flora and fauna. When it comes time for transportation improvement projects in those areas, government staff should give them the highest level of scrutiny.

The Amherst salamander tunnel under construction TOM TYNING PHOTO

The Amherst tunnels serve as an excellent model to follow, and there are others. The state of Florida went all out to create a series of tunnels called the ecopassage. Located in Paynes Prairie State Preserve in Allachua County, a two-mile-long wall diverts wildlife traveling across U.S. 441 into eight individual tunnels measuring between three and eight feet wide. The tunnels allow a wide variety of animals to pass, ranging from Florida water snakes to bobcats. Prior to construction, a study revealed that in one year, 2,411 animals were found dead in the road. After the tunnels were put in place, that number dropped to 157. This excluded the numbers of treefrogs found dead, which was substantial both before and after. They have a tendency to jump over the barriers. However, a good number of them were diverted to the tunnels, thus reducing their mortality rate as well. And, of those 157 killed after the barriers were installed, most were located beyond the two-mile diversion wall.

What impresses me are the fifty-one species utilizing these passageways: fish (9), salamanders (2), frogs (11), alligators (1), turtles (4), lizards (1), snakes (11), and mammals (12).

Much of the above work was made possible by the Transportation Equity Act for the 21st Century, which is under the U.S. Department of Transportation's Federal Highway Administration which states, "The TEA-21 offers an unprecedented opportunity for us to reduce highway impacts on wildlife. In our 1999 Strategic Plan, we commit ourselves to environmental stewardship—to protecting and enhancing the natural environment and communities affected by highway transportation. In the Plan, we also pledge to build and strengthen the partnerships that enable this to happen."

Because taking action to reduce road mortality can seem daunting when considering something as immense as a state highway, it is good to know that there is an agency whose job it is to oversee such things. I would suggest we let them know people are out there noticing some of the good work being done, and we should continue to fill them in on our areas of concern. They have money to spend, our money, to deal with this overwhelming problem. You can contact them at 202-366-0660, or visit their Web site at www.fhwa.dot.gov/environment/wildlifecrossings to see what is going on in your state.

It appears that salamander tunnels are popping up with greater frequency. There is one at Massachusetts Audubon's Wachusett Meadow

Sanctuary in Princeton. Five were constructed (for the Threatened Jefferson salamander) just north of Toronto in Canada. Recently, California tiger salamanders were given a tunnel on the grounds of Stanford University to make their journey less perilous. Officials and biologists at the university created a fifty-foot-long tunnel running from their upland habitat in Stanford Hills to their breeding grounds in Lake Lagunita. The tunnel lets the salamanders avoid the treacherous trip across the Junipero Serra Boulevard, where traffic was responsible for killing a couple hundred of them every year. The California tiger salamander, an attractive critter, black with heavy pearly-white markings, is listed as a "species of special concern" in the state. It is believed there are no more than 2,500 left. As with the Amherst tunnel, consideration had to be given to steering the animals to the tunnel entrance. To do this, Stanford built a barrier, this one made of asphalt, along the side of the road to channel the salamanders to where they need to go. It intercepts them at the bottom of a hill and turns them toward the entrance, where another barrier within catches them. Openings along the top of the tunnel can be seen from the road, and they allow in enough light to show the salamanders they are not entering a dead end.

Another strategy is being utilized that sounds so simple, it elicits a slap to the forehead with the response, "Now why didn't I think of that?" Road closures. Closing down roads to all but necessary traffic during the key migration nights can have a tremendous beneficial effect on the amphibians. In many cases, a particular road is not the only way for people to get from point A to point B. Blocking off such roads to through traffic can be, at worst, an inconvenience to those who want to get to where they are going in less time. Keep in mind, too, that most closures would only be necessary on rainy nights, and only for the week or so necessary for the frogs and salamanders to get to and from their breeding grounds.

I just read a story in the paper about a man who convinced the supervisor of the Delaware Water Gap National Recreation Area to shut down a road during amphibian migration. Closing this road in March has turned what was once an annual vehicular slaughter zone for up to 700 frogs and salamanders into an area of safe passage. This measure of amphibian protection has been occurring in Europe for decades. We have some catching up to do in this area. While pulling together the support and resources to construct migration tunnels under our roads may seem overwhelming for most citizens, getting your local government to temporarily shut down a road may bring quicker and less expensive success. For state roads, you can write your state agency for transportation planning to express your concern about the rapid loss of wildlife habitat to new-road construction and roadway expansion. Encourage it to incorporate wildlife considerations into future transportation planning and the renovation of existing roadways. Ask them what they are doing to reduce the wildlife mortality on the roads they create.

On a more local level, you can let your selectmen or mayor know your concerns and petition to have certain roads closed to through traffic during migration times. Naturally, access would have to be allowed for the homeowners on such roads. I am sure that most of them would not object to your petitioning for *less* traffic racing past their houses.

Tom Tyning believes it is important that we protect these small, local populations of frogs and salamanders. I couldn't agree more. While spotted salamanders and wood frogs are not endangered in our part of the world, we should bear in mind that if we keep chipping away at their habitats, what many now take for granted as a common species may not always remain so.

❧ 4 ❧

Frogsicles

WHEN THE BOSTON Red Sox's Ted Williams died on July 5, 2002, talk of his long baseball career was overshadowed by the attempts of his son, John Henry, to have his father's head put on ice. John Henry prevailed, and The Splendid Splinter's body is currently hanging upside down in a steel tank, accompanied by, but no longer attached to, his head. He joins approximately one hundred other souls in the United States who have opted for the possibility of a postdeath reunion upon the thawing of their cryonically preserved heads, and in some cases, bodies. (Contrary to popular belief, Walt Disney will not be among them; he has been cremated, and his remains are resting in Glendale, California.)

Mankind has long sought to escape mortality. However, the closest we have come to achieving this is through the belief in an afterlife, as offered up in many religions. It was generally accepted that once the physical body went, it was not coming back. While some religions speak of men and women rising from the dead while still on this earth, it is not something most of us expect to achieve.

Ironically, it was a Catholic priest, who, while questioning what life really is, introduced the possibility of cheating death. In 1940, Father Basil Luyet wrote *Life and Death at Low Temperatures*. In this work, he describes the experiments he conducted on freezing living cells. Luyet observed that while most cells were permanently destroyed upon freezing, some could be restored. It was his belief that the presence of life in an organism could live apart from that organism. This led him to the observation that there was another category of life called "latent life." While scientists had discussed the concept of a latent life since the eighteenth century, here was proof of it on a cellular level. In this state, an organism can exist in suspended animation for an extended period of time. As an example, Father (and Doctor) Luyet cited the phenomenon of nematode worms, which after spending years in a dried state, could be brought back to life by adding some water to them.

Luyet's work eventually led to a new area of science called cryobiology—cryo from the Greek word *kryos*, meaning frost. This began in Britain, where scientists were able to freeze red blood cells and bull semen and bring them back to a functioning state after thawing. They discovered that if the cells were soaked in glycerol, the damage caused by ice crystals would be minimized.

I can almost picture a wood frog reading this report and saying, "Duh!" Wood frogs, along with spring peepers and gray treefrogs, are categorized as being freeze tolerant.

There are basically three ways to deal with cold in the wild. One is to migrate, as evidenced by the southerly movement of birds every fall. Another is to hibernate, that is, to ride it out in a place that is less cold than the surrounding environs. And the last strategy is to tolerate it. We humans, along with a majority of living things on this planet, usually opt for the first two. We employ a strategy known as freeze avoidance. I am typing this on a damp, overcast, icy March morning. It's one of those mornings where the cold settles into your bones and the house just can't quite provide enough heat to chase it out. I took a hot shower to reactivate my core heat. Mornings like this make the thought of a creature freezing solid downright chilling. But lots of living things do this, ranging from plants and insects to mollusks and garter snakes. Naturally, some accomplish this feat better than others, the true ice kings and queens being the wood frogs.

This is not to say that some people out there are not without a semblance of freeze-tolerance skills. On November 27, 2000, magician David Blaine attempted to break the world record of fifty-seven hours encased in ice. To prepare, he immersed himself in a tub of ice for hours at a time. He also practiced sleeping standing up, not an easy feat. Prior to the encasing, he fasted for four days to clear out his system. On the morning of his stunt, he arrived in New York's Times Square dressed only in a pair of shorts, shirt, hat, and boots and instructed his assistants to encase him between two three-ton blocks of ice. Scores of onlookers, many communicating via messages scrawled on paper, offered encouragement. Blaine could only nod or shake his head in response.

Sixty-one hours, forty minutes, and fifteen seconds later, a visibly weak and pain-ridden Blaine exited the ice; he had indeed broken the record. But, while this was truly a remarkable display of cold tolerance (and, I might add, of standing in one place), it doesn't compare to what occurs within the true freeze-tolerant species. For example, while Blaine was encased, doctors kept a close monitor on his body core temperature; it never dipped below ninety-seven degrees. A ninety-seven-degree day is rather warm. In truly freeze-tolerant species, more than half of their body fluids turn to ice. If you pick up a wood frog that is in the middle of this stage and drop it on the floor, it will sound like you dropped a wooden block.

About fifteen years ago, I came across one of those wooden-block frogs. An overnight shift in the weather pattern had caused the temperature to drop in the double digits to about two below zero Fahrenheit. I was indoors on that frigid January afternoon, looking out the window at sparrows kicking up the leaves beneath my bird feeder when I noticed that one of them wasn't moving. I went outside to investigate and found that the sparrow was, in fact, a wood frog. It sat on the ground, unmoving; its eyes were hazy and seemingly lifeless. I picked up the frog and was startled by how cold and solid it was. At the time, I assumed it had frozen to death, but now I know this may not have been the case. What probably happened was that the frog was out and about in the relatively warmer weather prior to the cold front and took shelter beneath the leaf litter at its onset. The birds must have uncovered it in their foraging. (Fortunately, for the wood frog, I put it in the leaf litter on the side of the yard, so it may have pulled through.)

Here in the Northeast, we have three species of frogs that can be used to cool a winter cocktail: the wood frog, the spring peeper, and the gray treefrog. While all three do seek some form of shelter, or hibernaculum, to ride out the coldest of weather, they don't put as much thought into it as do their non-freeze-tolerant cousins. For example, green frogs and leopard frogs spend the winter on the pond or lake floor, below the freezing level. If the pond were to freeze down to the bottom, they'd be goners. This happens sometimes, and finding dead, bloated frogs in the spring is not uncommon. It's known as winterkill. But most of them do make it. They have the ability to slow their metabolism and body functions to a near standstill. Salamanders seek out burrows in the ground to get as far away from the surface as possible. Redback salamanders do, too, but they don't go as deep. The sugars in their body keep their fluids from freezing, and they can be active throughout the winter, but only on warmer days.

In contrast, the three freeze-tolerant frogs overwinter just below the leaf litter, or under rocks and logs, right smack in the path of the oncoming frost line. The fluids in their bodies drop in temperature to a supercooled state, but once their skin comes in contact with ice crystals, they begin to turn to ice themselves.

One may wonder why creatures would evolve to subject themselves to this harsh treatment, especially when so many others have found what would seem to be a more desirable alternative. What could be gained in allowing the body to transform to a helpless frozen state? We have to assume that that there are advantages to this adaptation, because mechanisms that fail get weeded out of the gene pool. So, advantages exist. For one, the ability to withstand colder temperatures allows for range expansion, which is why you can find wood frogs above the Arctic Circle. Also, the ability to deal with the harshest of weather without the need to seek out elaborate shelter must have allowed the freeze tolerant to survive when the freeze-avoiding species couldn't. It probably began that way. Some frogs got caught out in the cold, froze for a short time, and survived. Over time, those hardier frogs passed on that helpful trait to their progeny, which, in turn, grew even more adept at it. The wood frog under my bird feeder comes to mind. Had it been a bullfrog, it may not have survived that sudden change in temperature.

Another big plus for the freeze tolerant is that they get a head start on the breeding season. Being closer to the surface, they are the first to notice the warming weather. Air temperature changes more rapidly than water temperature, so they're out carousing and whooping it up while the others are slumbering beneath them. For the wood frogs, which utilize vernal pools, it is essential they get going early. Their tadpoles need to develop *before* their habitat dries out. Painted turtles also freeze solid. For them, the advantage comes in the form of predator avoidance. The hatchling turtles spend their first winter beneath the ground in a somewhat dormant state. This is a period in their life when there is little they could do to avoid being eaten by a host of creatures. Since it is winter, their food source does not allow for rapid growth, so they wait it out in their frozen little shells. As they grow, and develop better predator avoidance strategies, they lose the ability to freeze.

Before these animals could undergo freezing (and then come out of it again), certain problems had to be solved within their bodies. The main problem had to do with the elimination, or reduction, of damage to their cells. Freezing and thawing is an area we are still working out within our own species. Ice crystals wreak havoc on cells. They sap them of moisture, rob them of oxygen and nutrients, reduce their volume, and break the membranes. While icing down organs helps preserve them for transplants, those organs can only be kept in this state for a day or two. Once the ice crystals begin to form, capillaries are ruptured and cells are destroyed. While we are getting better at preserving body parts, we still have to fight the onset of ice formation inside them. In the cryogenic field, they now vitrify the brain, turning it into a glasslike state, which introduces fewer ice crystals. It is cooled down to the temperature of liquid nitrogen minus 190 degrees centigrade. This still causes fractures in the brain, but the cryogenicists believe that these would be easier to repair than what occurs from ice crystal damage.

A number of strategies allow freeze-tolerant species to survive the winter. They've developed adaptations to control the rate of freezing, where freezing occurs in the body, changes in cell volume, jump-starting of the metabolism, and surviving anoxia, or the reduction of oxygen.

Let's start with the first one, rate of freezing. In order for everything to work properly, a frog needs time to adjust and compensate for the onslaught of ice crystals within its body. Antifreeze, in the form of glucose in wood frogs and spring peepers, and alcohol in gray treefrogs, is produced in the liver. The liver sends these solutions to other vital organs in the body. If the freezing occurs before the glucose or alcohol can be dispensed, the frog will not recover. The ability to actually stimulate freezing within the body, by the use of ice-creating proteins, allows for some control. This could give them an edge when caught unawares by a sudden freeze.

Equally important is *where* the freezing takes place. As I mentioned earlier, more than fifty percent of a frog's body freezes solid. In some cases, up to sixty-five percent freezes. The freezing that takes place is extracellular, or outside of the cells, and it happens in a specific sequence. The ice crystals begin to form along the length of the muscle fibers. At this point, the frog's not going anywhere, as the muscles are now inflexible. Then the ice grows inside the abdominal cavity, and around, but not within, the organs. The freezing is also traveling from the base of the spine up to the brain, which keeps the brain functioning for as long as possible. Then major organs, such as the lungs and heart, become solid, until the very last organ, the liver, succumbs to the advancing intraherpetofaunial glacier (ice in the frog). Again, the liver has to be last, because it is doling out the antifreeze to where it is needed.

While all this is taking place, the organs and cells are dispelling water, sequestering it in other areas of the body. This prevents the physical damage that would occur from ice growing within. Here is another area where we have a problem in human cryogenics. When the cells expel this water, their volume is decreased dramatically. Cells can only shrink so much before they are destroyed. Mammalian cells lack the ability to soak up glucose or alcohol at a fast enough pace to arrest freeze damage. The freeze-tolerant frogs are somehow able to maintain that minimum cell volume, preventing those cells from going past the point of no return. This helps protect the cell membranes, which, in freeze-avoiding animals, would rupture under the stress of the extracellular ice. The cells also need to maintain the ability to function, that is, to transport water and solubles between components within and without the cells. To do this, they employ other forms of antifreeze around the membranes.

●

None of this would make any difference if the frog lacked the mechanisms to reverse direction and come back to life. For example, if I curled up under the leaf litter to wait out the winter in below zero temperatures, I would freeze solid, too. That's no great feat. My body would even make adjustments to decrease the damage caused by the cold. However, those adjustments would only buy me a minimal amount of time before I succumbed to the inevitable. Upon thawing, I'd stand no more chance of sitting up than does a chicken cutlet defrosting in a microwave.

The first parts to thaw within the frogs are the vital organs, such as the brain, heart, lungs, and kidneys. These areas held the highest concentrations of cryoprotectants (glucose or alcohol) during the freeze episode. The kidneys held the most, so they are the first to defrost. The brain is next, which is followed by the heart and then the lungs. This is the reverse order of the freezing that took place, which makes sense. The hierarchy of importance is going to dictate the last to be turned off and the first to be turned back on. Another reason the organs are able to thaw before the rest of the body, which seems illogical because most frozen objects thaw from the outside in, is due to the smaller amount of water in relation to the solid particulates within. Remember, these organs shed a considerable amount of water during the freezing, and the solids in those organs became less diluted. The area surrounding them is pretty much pure ice. An ice cube filled with sand will melt faster than an ice cube of pure water because there's a smaller percentage to melt.

Once the heart is pumping, blood is sent to the skin. Since frogs take in oxygen through this organ, this action most likely provides the first dose of the vital gas to the oxygen-starved body. This is followed by the lungs being switched on, and then finally, the muscles.

The sudden introduction of oxygen to cells starved of this vital gas for so long could also be fatal, as it creates a deluge of reactive oxygen species, or free radicals, within the body. These are unstable molecules that cause a chain reaction of instability as they attempt to balance themselves by robbing electrons from nearby molecules. All animals have to maintain a defense against free radicals, but the freeze-tolerant frogs have an abundance of high antioxidant enzymes to counter the sudden burst of oxygen in the body.

Oxygen attack is not the only problem to contend with. Although the bodies of these animals have adapted to deal with freezing and thawing, it is inevitable that some damage will occur, especially to the more delicate capillaries and tissues. It seems that while the frog is in suspended animation, it holds in reserve, within that all-important liver, a protein known as fibrinogen. This is sent through the plasma to aid in clotting, which keeps the frog from bleeding to death, and is believed to play a role in repairing some of the damage as well.

One of the final acts of shaking off the effects of the freeze is the removal of the excess glucose from the body. The glucose begins to accumulate in the fall and is present in high levels prior to the freezing weather. In most vertebrates, hyperglycemia (excess sugars in the blood) is detrimental to the metabolism. Diabetes is a form most of us are familiar with. Once the frog is out of danger of being frozen, that excess sugar coursing through its veins is unnecessary, and unhealthy, so it's cleared out of the system. Here is another area where these amphibians excel and where we could use more proficiency.

•

Prior to the appearance of creatures able to let winter wash over them, desiccation, or dehydration, was the key concern. Terrestrial life did not evolve beneath the snowpack; it radiated from the warm seas and lakes to the surrounding land. Water was, and still is, key to survival. However, once those pioneering terrestrials left their aquatic habitats, they left behind the only sure way to keep their whistles wet. However, there were enough advantages, as stated in the chapter titled "From Amphibians to Us," to risk the chances of not finding enough water to stay alive. It is believed that the adaptations that evolved to prevent desiccation are what eventually led to the ability to freeze solid. Those adaptations most likely started out as a response to periodic drying of lakes and ponds and eutrophication (low oxygen conditions). Those that didn't dry out or die of anoxia kept their species moving forward. When they touched down on land, they already had some way to deal with these conditions, which improved over time. I can see a correlation between the reaction to desiccation and the expansion into cooler climates. Cold air tends to be drier than warm air. Anyone with eczema can tell you winter is the toughest time, as the lack of moisture in the air causes the skin to dry out. Partly this is due to our heated homes, but the outdoors offers little respite. Cold air simply does not do a good job of holding moisture.

In a paper titled "Natural Freezing Survival in Animals," Kenneth and Janet Storey write about an experiment conducted with wood frogs and spring peepers. Both species were subjected to controlled, whole-body dehydration to the point where they each lost between fifty and sixty percent of total body water. Both species responded with rapid production of glucose in the liver and the export of that glucose to the other organs. This response to drying out is nearly identical to the response of freezing. When the frogs were rehydrated, their glucose levels fell, as they do when they thaw. Interestingly, when they tried the same experiment with freeze-intolerant frogs, specifically leopard frogs, the response was the same. The glucose levels in the liver rose twenty-four-fold. However, in the peepers, which are freeze tolerant, that level rose sixty-fold and in the wood frog, a whopping three-hundred-thirteen-fold. So, while the leopard frogs' response was similar, it was not nearly as great in magnitude. This could explain why they cannot cut it as a freeze-tolerant species. Their glucose levels just don't get high enough to protect the organs.

This experiment led the Storeys to conclude: "Thus, although the magnitude of the dehydration induced hyperglycemia (increased glucose production) is much lower in *R. pipiens* (leopard frog) than the freeze-tolerant species, the glycogenolytic response to dehydration is clearly in place in the freeze-intolerant species, and this suggests that the cryoprotectant response to freezing grew out of a more primitive hyperglycemic response to dehydration."

They also pointed out that as with the wood frogs and spring peepers, which protect their organs from freezing to the very end, priority was given to defending the water content in the organs of the leopard frogs. The pools surrounding these organs were first to lose the water. In fact, even when sixty percent of their fluid was removed, the water volume in the liver remained unchanged. This would be key to taking the next step in regulating the release of glucose at the onset of freezing.

So, for now, the leopard frogs, and the other freeze-intolerant frogs, need to preserve the liquid state of their body fluids. As do the salamanders, although there is one, the Siberian newt, that can freeze, thanks again to nature's sugary gift of glucose. Perhaps, over time, other frogs will develop the ability to freeze. The mechanisms are in place; they are just not quite up to the job. I can't help but think about all those pickerel and green frogs I come across on late winter/early spring rainy nights when it's still really cold. And *they* are really cold, too; I've seen them sitting on ice-covered ponds. It seems they, too, live right on the edge of our coldest season. I am sure that they can, like garter snakes, and certain lizards and turtles, survive a very brief freezing. I am also sure that they could benefit from range and season extension. But, maybe the benefits have not been compelling enough. The fact that many of these freeze-intolerant species can allow their body fluids to supercool, that is, go to a temperature below freezing without turning to ice, is an impressive trick in itself—one that must have cryogenic scientists saying, "If only. . ."

As for me, when the frog frost is upon us, I'll just keep turning up the heat in the house and throwing on a few more layers before heading outdoors. And when I'm gone, if someone tries to freeze my head, once that ice cream headache subsides, I'm coming after the person who did it! (Well, assuming I have a *body*. . .)

❧ 5 ❧

Amphibians and Us

IN 1970, Harper & Row published Arnold Lobel's Caldecott Honor children's book, *Frog and Toad Are Friends.* Frog is the upbeat doer, tall and green, dressed in a pair of pants and an open jacket. Toad, easily frustrated by life's little problems, enjoys his sleep. ("Blah" is his reaction to Frog's enthusiastic announcement that spring has at last arrived.) He is short, squat, and a golden brown. He, too, wears a pair of pants and a jacket. What sets him apart as a toad is the poison-bearing parotoid gland Lobel included on the back of his character's neck. (Frog is instead sporting a tympanic membrane.) They live in a verdant world, the greens muted by browns and pale orange. It is a place shared with snails, birds, raccoons, and other creatures one may expect to find in pond, field, and forest.

I first came upon *Frog and Toad Are Friends*, and the two sequels, while working as a page for the Commack Library in Long Island, New York. I was in my second year of college at the time and my job at the library was to shelve books in the children's section. There, I came across many of the classics—*Where The Wild Things Are, The Chronicles of Narnia, A Wrinkle In Time*, and Lobel's *Frog and Toad* books. I was immediately drawn into the little world he had created. The simple lives of Frog and Toad showed the joys and rewards of friendship. Who wouldn't want to be their friends and live in that world? The illustrations were done back in the days of pre-separated color production, a complicated technique where the artist doesn't see the results of his or her labors until the pages are printed. Using a palette of various shades of gray to represent the colors red, yellow, blue, and black, Lobel managed to put his characters into an earthy and lush green-brown setting. I loved those colors. I wanted to paint using those colors, and since the college I was attending was the School of Visual Arts, I had plenty of opportunity to do so.

The stories of Frog and Toad had a tremendous influence on my ensuing career. Lobel's book was the perfect example of how someone with an interest in writing stories *and* painting pictures could combine the two.

I enrolled in a children's book illustration class in my fourth year, and by the end of the class and my college years, I signed my first book contract with Dial Press for a children's book called *Talester the Lizard*.

Twenty-five years after first coming across these two famous amphibians, I still find myself smiling when I leaf through their book.

There is another famous toad in children's literature. He is a prominent player in Kenneth Grahame's *The Wind in the Willows*, published in 1908. Mr. Toad is a self-confident, good-natured, well off (but not a millionaire) amphibian with a love for driving. The problem is that he isn't very good at it. In fact, he crashes many an elegant motorcar. When Badger asks, "How many has he had?" Toad's friend Rat can't just give a simple answer:

> "Smashes, or machines?" asked the Rat. "Oh, well, after all, it's the same thing—with Toad. This is the seventh. As for the others—you know that coach-house of his? Well, it's piled up—literally piled up to the roof—with fragments of motorcars, none of them bigger than your hat! That accounts for the other six—so far as they can be accounted for."

Toad's poor driving eventually leads to his arrest and an intervention staged by his friends to convince him to give up motorcars. He goes along with them so they will leave him alone long enough for him to get back to his next motorcar.

Aside from the stoats, which invade Toad's ancestral home, Toad Hall, the characters really don't carry a lot of the attributes of the animals they are supposed to be. Okay, the mole is shy and the rat is clever and the stoats are weaselly, but Mr. Toad, or "Toady," is basically a human dressed in a toad suit. He is actually based on Grahame's son, Alistair, who suffered from certain excesses of behavior. Mr. Toad's adventures and misfortunes first appeared in letters from father to son. Grahame had hoped Alistair could take lessons from the affable amphibian that thought so little of consequences, but Alistair's troubles ran too deeply to be purged by a wild cast of allegorical players. Prior to his twentieth birthday, he committed suicide by jumping in front of a train.

When I think of real live toads, the human traits that come to mind are laziness (they spend a lot of time sitting still), grumpiness (that bulldog face), and maybe a small dose of naiveté (again, the face). Mr. Toad may be described as naive, and in a way, brave. Toads look like they could be brave, when they care to be. I imagine them as beer drinkers, by the way, partial

A stout-drinking, cigar-smoking, ready-to-jump-into-a-fight face, if ever I saw one

to a bitter ale, or perhaps a good dark stout, and they won't put up with crap from anyone. While they don't go out of their way to look for trouble, they won't hesitate to jump in when it presents itself. In fact, they may even, on occasion, play the reluctant hero. If they smoke, it's a cigar—a big one that smells bad.

Mr. Toad, or more specifically, the 1949 Disney movie *The Wind in the Willows*, was the inspiration for the Disneyland/Disney World attraction "Mr. Toad's Wild Ride." It was a fairly slow-moving ride, lasting about two minutes, in which you blast through haystacks and a fireplace, and nearly run people over. I rode it once more than a decade ago, and I have to admit that it was one of the more boring rides in the park. However, Disney's plan to scrap it caused a large movement to save it. Web sites devoted to its preservation sprung up everywhere. Green-shirted protesters staged "Mr. Toad Ins" at the site itself. Disney was not swayed. In 1998, after forty-three years in operation, "Toad's Wild Ride" was replaced by the "Many Adventures of Winnie the Pooh."

While Frog and Toad and Mr. Toad may lay claim to being the best-known amphibians in modern literature, there's a frog out there in Hollywood with world renown on the screen. He's a bright green, button-eyed creature that goes by the name of Kermit. Despite his great fame, he still retains that approachable coolness—that *frogginess*. The Jim Henson creation first appeared on television in 1955, on a five-minute show called *Sam and Friends*. He looked more like an anole (lizard) back then and didn't really become a frog until his appearance in the TV special *Hey, Cinderella*. It was his stint as a reporter on *Sesame Street* that gave him his first exposure to a large audience. The frog's everyman attitude, dry humor, and high throaty voice appealed to people. It seemed perfectly natural to forget he was a puppet—Muppet, actually—and to believe he was a talking frog. (Had Jim Henson made Kermit a squirrel or a cat, he would have never gotten as far.) He has since become the most recognizable frog on the planet, appearing in everything from his own movies to *Hollywood Squares*.

One of Kermit's most memorable roles was as the title character in the Jacob and Wilhelm Grimm story, *The Frog Prince*. It was originally published in 1812, in a collection of tales called *Kinder-und Hausmärchen*. The story tells of three thirsty princesses who, one by one, go to the well to get a drink. When they lift the glass from the water, they discover it is cloudy. A frog pops up and says, "If you will be my sweetheart, dear, then I will give you water clear."

The third princess agrees to this and lets the amorous frog join her in bed. Like the stereotypical womanizer throughout the ages, he's gone before the sun's shining through the window. He returns later that evening to jump back in the sack with the princess. On the third day, he comes back as a handsome prince. (I guess she paid her dues.)

Within this same collection of stories, Jacob and Wilhelm included another story called *The Frog King*. It has the same ending as *The Frog Prince*, but this one begins with one princess, not three, who drops her ball in the water. The frog offers to retrieve it for her if she promises to let him sit next to her at dinner, eat off her plate, and then join her in the ol' boudoir. She agrees, thinking he'll never call her on it, but he does, and the king compels her to keep her promises.

So, there he is, in the beautiful princess's bed. He pulled it off, but she is so revolted by the sight of this slimy thing lying next to her that she picks him up and slams him into the wall. The battered frog slides down and plops into her bed where he is transformed into a handsome prince. Then, they get it on royally (or so it's implied).

In 1823, Edgar Taylor wrote an English translation of the Grimm stories and published them in his book, *German Popular Stories*. His version of *The Frog Prince* is the one with which we are most familiar, a combination of Grimm's *The Frog King* and *The Frog Prince*. The story begins as in *The Frog King* and ends as in *The Frog Prince*. Taylor omitted the part where she slams the frog into the wall, though, thinking it too violent for English tastes.

The point of the story, I believe, was not to illustrate the propensity of frogs to talk young ladies into bed, but to show that what may be unappealing on the outside can have true beauty on the inside.

Another well-known collector of fables, Aesop, wrote of frogs in *The Frogs' Complaint Against the Sun*:

> Once upon a time, when the Sun announced his intention to take a wife, the Frogs lifted up their voices in clamor to the sky. Jupiter, disturbed by the noise of their croaking, inquired the cause of their complaint. One of them said, "The Sun, now while he is single, parches up the marsh, and compels us to die miserably in our arid homes. What will be our future condition if he should beget other suns?"

What is it about frogs that so appeals to our popular culture? People collect them, write children's books about them, and sing songs about them. They are generally regarded as interesting to look at and are often viewed as comical figures. I suppose that frogs do have smart-alecky faces. The eyes, though conspicuously displayed on top of the head, appear to be squinting. This lends to the impression that they are thinking, or just kicking back. Salamanders lack that attribute, which may explain why we see so few of them in our icons. People notice eyes. This may have something to do with ours being placed in such a visible position on the front of our head. We are aware when a person refuses to meet our eyes, and become uncomfortable when stared at for too long. In the frog, we have an animal with a pair of eyes that jump right out at you. If you were to give a child a crayon and ask him to draw a frog, the drawing will most likely start out as two large orbs.

Add to those knowing, half-closed eyes a contented grin, and you have a creature that can be assumed to have all kinds of things knocking around in its head. The grin is just that, too—contented, not a big goofy smile. It is almost like the famous grin worn about three inches beneath the lidded eyes of DaVinci's *Mona Lisa*. For centuries, we have pondered the meaning behind that smile. A frog's smile can be equally intriguing—slow and easy,

A frog, kicking back . . .

like their posture. Frogs don't stand. Frogs don't sit. They squat, and they are always, in the military vernacular, at ease.

Then there is that whole naked aspect of frogs. Mammals hide behind a mat of fur, insects are covered with armor, and birds with feathers. Frogs don't wear anything. They don't need no stinkin' fur, armor, feathers, or clothes. They venture out in their altogether. The world is their nudist camp, and the lakes and ponds are their swimming pools.

In 1955, Chuck Jones, the prolific animator and director, drew one of those naked frogs. Well, it wasn't completely naked. He gave it a top hat. The frog's name was Michigan J. Frog, and he is the very same character that dances across the WB logo on television. His first name, Michigan, probably comes from "The Michigan Rag," a song he sang in his six-minute debut. His middle initial, J, could have just been furthering the tradition many cartoon writers employ when giving their characters middle initials: Bullwinkle J. Moose, Rocky J. Squirrel, Phineas J. Whoopie, Elmer J. Fudd, Homer J. Simpson, and so on. It's also possible some of those Js could be a tip of the hat to some of the talent behind the scenes.

Michigan J. Frog appeared in one animated short on December 31, 1955. Michael Maltese, who had written a number of television cartoons throughout the 1940s and 1950s, penned it. To refresh your memory, the story, *One Froggy Evening*, is about a construction worker who discovers a frog in the cornerstone of a demolished building. To his great surprise and elation, the frog immediately begins a song and dance routine, complete with top hat and cane. Attempts to turn this discovery into a windfall are thwarted, however, by the frog's refusal to sing for anyone else. In the end, the man is left penniless from his unsuccessful attempts to break into show biz.

While many may remember this cartoon, I'm sure that relatively few know that it is loosely based on a real event. In July 1897, a hollow marble cornerstone was set in place for a courthouse in Eastland, Texas. Within that cornerstone were a bible and a few other knickknacks. Will Wood, son of justice of the peace Ernest Wood, had, for some reason, brought a horned toad (which is actually a lizard) with him to the event. In a stroke of mischievous spontaneity, Ernest dropped the lizard into the marble block. The block was sealed and buried under three stories of building.

On February 8, 1928, the building was once again demolished to make way for a new one. Three thousand people turned out to see the opening of the time capsule. A man reached in, pulled out a dusty old horny toad, and held it up. Suddenly it began to twitch—first one leg, and then the other. Soon, it was fully awake and raring to go, and the crowd went wild.

The lizard was named Old Rip after Rip Van Winkle, and became a huge national celebrity. He went on tour throughout the United States and even got to meet President Calvin Coolidge. About a year later, he died of pneumonia and is currently on display, laid in state in a velvet-lined coffin at the Eastland courthouse.

•

Speaking of bigger-than-life frogs, a few years ago, Betsy and I had gone for a drive to the northeast corner of Connecticut to find an antique window for our shed. On our way down Route 66 in Windham County, we came across two pairs of giant (eleven-foot) frogs sitting guard at the Thread City Crossing, or Frog Bridge, at Route 32. Judging from the ridge wrapping around the tympanic membrane, I surmised these were bullfrogs. They sat on spools of thread that were meant to represent Willimantic's historical place in the manufacture of cotton thread. It turns out they're there to commemorate a somewhat embarrassing event in the town's history—the Windham Frog Fight of 1754.

Between 1750 and 1754, we (we being the British colonies) were having a bit of trouble with the French. Territorial disputes were growing, forts were being built, troops were mobilizing, and skirmishes were being fought. While war would not officially be declared until 1756, the colonists were a bit on edge.

In the town of Windham, Connecticut, Colonel Eliphalet Dyer had pulled together a regiment to mobilize against the enemy. In *Legendary Connecticut* (Curbstone Press, 1984), David E. Philips wrote:

One of Windham County's Frog Bridge sentinels

Then, on a dark, cloudy, steamy night in June, according to the most reliable witnesses, it happened. After family prayers had been duly performed, the residents of the settlement retired to rest, and for several hours all enjoyed a period of well-earned sleep. Just after midnight, however, their peaceful slumbers were abruptly ended by a noise so loud and hideous that they rose from their beds in one horrified mass of humanity.

The frightful clamor seemed to be coming from right over their heads and from all directions at once, a shrieking, clattering, thunderous roar such as never had been heard on earth before. To some it sounded like the yells and war whoops of attacking Indians. To others it was the last ding-dong of doom, announcing the arrival of Judgment Day. However, one elderly black man, wiser than his neighbors, was said to have protested that decision, arguing that the Day of Judgment could not occur at night. The general terror was increased when many villagers swore that they could distinguish particular names, like DYER and ELDERKIN [another local lawyer and militia colonel], reverberating, at intervals, across the heavens, as if in awful summons.

The militia, believing they were under attack by the Indians, took to battle. Aiming in the general direction of the clamor, they emptied their muskets into the darkness. They fought bravely throughout the night and come dawn, the sounds of the enemy abated. They had won, and nary a soul was lost to the enemy.

The elation felt by the townspeople was palpable. However, it was soon replaced by embarrassment. In searching the area for vanquished foes, they came upon the true source of the horrific sounds that brought them to arms. A couple miles from the town green was Colonel Dyer's pond. The pond was virtually dry as the result of a drought they had been experiencing. Strewn about its banks were scores and scores of dead bullfrogs. Apparently, in a desperate effort to claim the last remaining wet areas, the amphibians had engaged in a battle of their own. Their battle cries and dying moans must have reverberated beneath the cloud cover, carried further by the damp air.

Naturally, the Windhamites' battle made them the butt of many jokes for two hundred years. But in 2001, they showed that a town government could display humility and a sense of humor by completing the bridge commemorating the event. Artist Leo Jensen did a beautiful job on the sculptures, and I recommend a pilgrimage to see the bridge and the bronze tablet at Frog Pond where the massacre took place.

•

If this had happened outside one of the French garrisons, would they have turned the fiasco into a culinary *soiree*? The French have been so associated with this penchant for eating frogs that a favorite English nickname for them is Frogs. There are other suggestions for the origin of that name, but when you think of frog legs, you do think of French cuisine. Ironically, commercial frog harvesting has been illegal in France for more than thirty years as the result of pressure from environmental groups. Most of the frogs they do eat come from Indonesia. At one point, Bangladesh supplied most of the frog legs consumed here in the United States. However, the Bangladesh government soon found their country overrun with flies and put an end to the frog harvest. Leaving the frogs in place as fly control was far less expensive than controlling the insects with insecticides. The export of frogs is now banned in that country.

In the early 1900s, frog legs were not well regarded in England. A chef at London's Carlton Hotel thought this culinary prejudice was unwarranted and offered them on the menu as *cuisses de nymphes aurore*, French for "legs of the dawn nymphs." Apparently the name change was enough to make a frog eater even out of the Prince of Wales, who would never have considered consuming this fare.

I ate frog legs at my high school graduation dinner with my family in 1977. My brother Jim and I were trying to outdo each other in our meal orders. He ordered sweetbreads (calf's thymus gland) and I ordered the *cuisses de grenouilles*, or frog legs. There is no doubt that he won that one (or lost, depending on how you look at it).

Usually, only the upper joint of the hind leg is served, which has a single bone similar to the upper joint of a chicken wing. Frog legs are commonly prepared by deep-frying, broiling, or sautéing. In the United States, most of the frogs consumed are bullfrogs and green frogs. Bullfrogs have more meat and are the obvious choice. I remember commenting that it tasted somewhat like a fishy chicken and wasn't that bad. I haven't eaten them since, though, and it has nothing to do with that National Lampoon cartoon of the legless frog on a roller in a French restaurant.

●

While frogs have long been associated with the dinner plate, they've also been a part of Americana. In 1865, a young Samuel Clemens (Mark Twain) visited Angels Camp in the heart of California gold country. He sat by a stove with Ben Coon, a former Illinois River pilot, and listened as Ben told the story of a famous jumping frog. The story not only inspired Twain's "The Celebrated Jumping Frog of Calaveras County," but also aided in spreading the word of this sport throughout the world. Frog-jumping contests happen everywhere. The amphibian athletes, like the delicacy, are usually bullfrogs and, again, like the delicacy, are chosen for their ampleness of leg.

Rules vary, but the gist of it is that you draw a circle, put your frog in the middle, and the longest jumper is the winner. Sometimes only one jump is measured, and sometimes two or three are. A bullfrog, one that's in peak physical shape, can cover more than twenty feet in three hops. In Calaveras County, the annual frog jump is a huge event, drawing 40,000 people. As many as 2,000 bullfrogs are entered each year. This has been going on since 1928.

As with anything, there has been some controversy. Animal rights activists are concerned about the welfare and treatment of the frogs. They're not thrilled with the idea of taking wild animals from their habitats and using them as, well, toys. The Department of Fish and Game (DFG) is concerned about the impact that releasing the frogs back into the wild could have on native populations of frogs. It has been standard practice and encouraged tradition to return the amphibians back to their respective ponds. However, bullfrogs, while native to the Northeast, are an introduced species in California. They are an aggressive and territorial lot that have wrought havoc upon the red-legged frogs, the native species that were used in Twain's book. Intermingling of all the contestants could also transfer froggy diseases that could in turn be transferred to native populations. It is against the law, and fineable up to $5,000, to release bullfrogs back into the wild.

This has created a potential dilemma for the county. The frog-jumping contest has been a huge economic boon to the area. People come from all over the world to watch and participate. Would the "frog jockeys" be required to kill their athletes upon completion of the contest? This would drop a discernable pall over the event.

The DFG recently found some kind of loophole to allow this contest to go on. While they have their job to do, and their concerns are legitimate, they didn't want to have to put the kibosh on such a popular event.

Interestingly, California is one of the few states with laws governing frog policy and frog-jumping contests:

> ARTICLE 6880. As used in this article, "frog-jumping contest" means a contest generally and popularly known as a frog-jumping contest, which is open to the public and is advertised or announced in a newspaper.
>
> ARTICLE 6881. Frogs to be used in frog-jumping contests shall be governed by this article only. Frogs to be so used may be taken at any time and without a license or permit.
>
> ARTICLE 6882. If the means used for taking such frogs can, as normally used, seriously injure the frog, it shall be conclusively presumed the taking is not for the purposes of a frog-jumping contest.
>
> ARTICLE 6883. Any person may possess any number of live frogs to use in frog-jumping contests, but if such a frog dies or is killed, it must be destroyed as soon as possible, and may not be eaten or otherwise used for any purpose.

Sigh. Nothing's easy.

The town of Rayne, in the middle of Louisiana Cajun country, is home to a little more than 8,500 people. This is a small town by most standards. Small as that it is, though, it boasts a pretty big claim—The Frog Capital of the World. Frogs are everywhere in Rayne. As you enter the town, you are immediately greeted by frogs painted on the underpass of Interstate 10. In town, they appear in murals on stores, schools, and even the police station. In addition to the forty or so murals on the buildings, frogs appear on trees, billboards, T-shirts, and street signs. The town also offers the annual Frog Festival, which has been taking place on Labor Day for more than three decades. Tens of thousands migrate to Rayne, Louisiana, to ride the rides, compete in the frog derbies, and to, perhaps, meet the reigning Frog Festival Queen in person.

The frog mania of Rayne goes back to the 1880s, when gourmet chef Donat Puchew sold his choice bullfrogs, along with other wild delectables, to New Orleans restaurants. There were many canals and wetlands in Rayne, so the frogs were plentiful. Jacques Weill, and his brothers, Edmond and Gautran, heard about this all the way over in France and settled in town to begin their own frog exporting business. It was wildly successful and responsible for the town's reputation as the frog capital of the world.

Rayne no longer exports frogs, because there aren't enough of them for it to be worthwhile anymore.

●

We have been sharing the world with amphibians throughout recorded and unrecorded history. Because we're large-brained creatures with huge imaginations and a tendency to try and make things fit into comfortable explanations, we've assigned many attributes and meanings to the creatures around us. It's no surprise that the unusual habits of an amphibian could inspire a wealth of conjecture and convince us to lend them powers beyond our own meager capabilities. The word *salamander*, for example, comes from the Greek word meaning "fire lizard." The ancients linked salamanders to fire because the amphibians often crawled out from logs that had been thrown onto fires, which led to the belief that salamanders could walk through fire. I'm sure that what they were witnessing, however, were salamanders hightailing it away due to an extreme *lack* of such ability.

In the ninth century, Baghdadi scientist and scholar Ibn Wahshiyya would have begged to differ with me. In his *Book on Poisons* he says that the salamander cannot only walk into a blazing fire and come out alive, but its "cold humor" extinguishes the flame. "This animal," he writes, "is one of the strange works of nature and a wonder of the stars' powers." Then he goes on to describe how to hunt this rare beast. Apparently you have to consume wine diluted in castoreum (beaver musk) and ambergris (a waxy mass from the intestines of a sperm whale), eat a sheep (feel free, he writes, to garnish with onions), slather pitch tar all over your naked body, and set a trap using a weasel as bait (mice work, too).

The amazing thing is that this is exactly what I do before going out looking for salamanders, and it works. In truth, I think there must have been easier ways to put out campfires, but I suppose the hunt was the thing.

•

The amphibian practice of skin eating has led to all kinds of far-reaching conjectures. Many frogs eat their shed skin. This recycles valuable nutrients and, perhaps, hides the evidence of their lingering in the vicinity. The Olmec tribes, who existed between 1300 and 400 B.C. in the eastern lowlands of Mexico, left behind carved images of their toad god of rebirth. The images portrayed a toadish deity devouring its own skin. They believed it was reborn by eating itself, and in doing so, perpetuated a cycle of death and rebirth, which trickles down to the people and nature below.

Their Aztec neighbors had a similar deity, Tlaltecuhti. Appearing in images as either a toadlike woman or a big toad, she was the Earth Mother goddess and embodied the cycle of death and rebirth. She is often depicted as squatting with her mouth open to take in the souls of the dead while simultaneously whelping new ones.

Then there's Ceneotl, another goddess of the pre-Colombian people. She was the patron of childbirth and fertility and was the oddest of creatures—a toad with udders.

Hekat, the Egyptian frog goddess

Ancient Egypt had a frog goddess, which was the symbol of fertility and, like the Olmec god, renewal. Heket was her name and like many of the Egyptian god images left behind, she had a human body and the head of the particular creature, in this case, a frog, whose powers it was believed to embody. Daughter of the Sun God Re and consort of Khnum, it was her charge to breathe the air of life into a child before it was placed in the womb of the soon-to-be mother. Frog amulets bearing her visage have been found, and they are believed to have been worn by women hoping to conceive. That a frog woman would be in charge of fertility could have something to do with the phenomenon of frog population explosion that followed the annual flooding of the Nile.

Even in modern times, the toad plays a role in bringing more people into the world. In a little mountain hamlet in Spain, a particular toad is believed to bear the same gifts as a dose of Viagra. Squatting over the village is a seventeen-square-foot outcropping of rock that looks like a giant toad. It is believed that anyone who touches it three times under a full moon will become a vigorous lover. Some claim to be instantly blessed by this ritual and immediately run home before that blessing wears off.

Not a bad little gift, but it's nothing compared to some others offered by the amphibians. In Asia, scholars wrote of a particular fungus that grew from the head of a toad. Consuming this fungus would give the gift of immortality. Why does the term *toad licking* come to mind?

Toad licking is real. In many species, particularly the Cane Toad (*Bufo marinus*) and the Sonoran Desert Toad (*Bufo alvarius*), the venom produced by the parotoid glands contains a psychoactive chemical called bufotenine. One way to partake of this elixir is to squeeze the toad to release the venom, and then give the skin a few licks. Another technique involves drying or crystallizing the venom and smoking it. This is the preferred method, so I hear. The effect has been likened to that of being strapped to the bottom of a jet as it takes off. I read one account where a toad licker watched in horror as his friend's face exploded into a million pieces. Another felt an intense love for all things and met God himself. Higher levels of intake cause the face to turn eggplant purple, an effect that, fortunately, wears off.

Toad venom is considered far more powerful than LSD or psylociben mushrooms. In the late 1960s, the U.S. Drug Enforcement Agency outlawed the possession and consumption of bufotenine. Since then, I believe the law has been enforced only once. And once again, Calaveras County was put on the map thanks to an amphibian, this time, the Sonoran desert toad. In 1994, Bob and Connie Shepard were arrested on drug charges after admitting they smoked the toads' venom. Their toads were seized and held as evidence by the drug task force. The Shepards faced up to fifteen years in jail, but were eventually let go with a lesser sentence.

While the Shepards may have been the first to be arrested for toad tripping, they were by no means the only ones out there partaking of the bufotoxin. Ironically, when the news of the law banning bufotoxin hit the media, it sparked a rash of toad lickings by folks who would never have even considered it. This is just one of the things that amuses me about the human animal. When told we can't do something, we want to do it even more. The law doesn't extend to dogs, which have also been known to lick the occasional Bufonidae when the opportunity presents itself. If it doesn't kill them, which happens on occasion, it leaves them pleasantly tipsy.

The venom of some frogs, particularly the poison dart frogs, has been used as a chemical weapon since prehistoric times. When threatened, these frogs release batrachotoxin, a nerve toxin, from glands just behind the ears. The actual toxin comes from the consumption of poisonous insects; if you were to deprive frogs of those bugs, they would not be able to produce their poison. The alkaloid has a bitter taste and a smell that has been described as peppery. The frogs carrying this defense are usually brightly colored, an attribute of many toxic biota from moths to plants. This gives the predator fair warning that the frog would be its last meal. It would do the frog no good if it were to kill the animal once it is ingested. This warning teaches would-be predators to steer clear of them in the future.

The native people of Central and South America would pick up the frogs with a leaf and rub the tip of their dart or arrow or spear on its back. The Choco people of Colombia still practice this today. Their weapon of

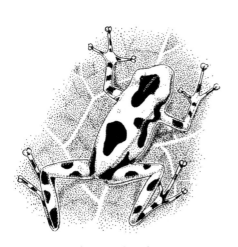

A poison dart frog

choice is the blowdart gun, and it's used to drop monkeys (their food) from the trees. The hunter pins the frog to the ground with a stick. He then drags his dart across the frog's back to coat it with the venom. Scientists in the area report they have come across treefrogs with black lines across their backs; those marks have come from the hunters.

The venomous attributes of frogs and toads were undoubtedly the basis for the long-held and widespread superstition of the toad stone. It was once believed that toads bore a jewel in their heads, and a human who possessed one could use it to detect the presence of poison. It would be worn around the neck in an amulet or around the finger as a ring. When the stone came in the proximity of poison, it would change color or grow warmer. Shakespeare makes mention of this in *As You Like It* and writes, "Sweet are the uses of adversity which, like the toad, ugly and venomous, wears yet a precious jewel in his head."

Toads often play the role of the villain. In John Milton's *Paradise Lost*, it is not a serpent who whispers to Eve, "Hey, check out those apples over there." It's a toad. Apparently Mr. Milton thought less of toads than he did of snakes.

In one of my early children's books, *Amanda and the Witch Switch*, I, too, cast the toad as the villain. Amanda just happened to be in such a good mood on a particular day that upon coming across a toad on a rock she

Illustration from Amanda and the Witch Switch

granted him three wishes. The toad didn't have to think long before requesting for his first wish that he be made into a witch himself. After she granted this wish, he then turned Amanda into a toad. When I speak to children in schools about how I arrived at this idea, I explain to them how it came from a sketch I'd done of a witch holding a toad in her hands. For some reason, I had given the toad kind of a wise-guy face. As mentioned earlier, that's how I envision toads. They're smart-asses, so all I had to do was figure out what kind of trouble he was going to cause. Naturally, since this is a children's book, he gets his comeuppance in the end.

We all hear negative connotations about toads when we're young. What's one of the first things we learn about them? If you touch one, you get warts. This piece of untruth obviously stems from the bumpy appearance of the supposed purveyor of this virus.

•

Amphibians surround us in both actuality and history. No matter what part of the world you travel to you will find tales of toads and frogs. They have been regarded as benefactors or omens of ill, and they have been both maligned and worshiped throughout the ages.

Next time you are outdoors on a moonlit night, look up at our glowing satellite and give a nod to the giant toad that looks down on us. In China, the man in the moon doesn't exist. The shadows they see are a toad. This female toad has a huge appetite, as evidenced by her occasional attempts to devour the moon, causing what we would call an eclipse. I use the pronoun "she" because of the toad's place in the Taoist philosophy of Yin-Yang, the symbol of the interplay of forces in the universe. In Chinese philosophy, yin and yang represent the two primal cosmic forces in the universe. Yin is the open, unresisting, cold female force; it is the moon goddess, the toad seen in the moon's shadow. The moon became the ultimate symbol of yin because it bears the face of a toad. She links water with darkness, darkness with the moon, and the moon with yin.

Prior to writing this chapter, I had stepped outdoors to see if I could find the toad in the moon. It helps if (a) you know where to look, and (b) you have a good imagination. It is located within the maria (dark sections of the moon) on the left side. The toad is seen at a three-quarters angle, as if you are looking at it from its right side. Its form takes up the entire shadowy area on the left. I actually find it easier to see the toad in the moon than the man in the moon.

When I look at the moon now, that toad jumps right out at me. I often

The toad in the moon

find myself smiling when I see it. I'm not even sure why. Maybe it has something to do with the cosmic forces having a sense of humor. When I observe toads and other frogs, I get a sense that Mother Nature had fun creating these grinning, gulping, hopping virtuosos of puddle and pond. To see one on the world's largest glowing billboard seems a worthy tip of the hat to them.

ᔄ 6 ᔄ

Springs and Slimys

A FEW SUMMERS ago I had a hankering. That's nothing new. People get hankerings all the time: for a big sandwich or a cool frothy one or to see a movie or to go out and smack a golf ball around. What I hankered for was to see something rare. Sometimes I just want to find something I've never found before, and usually that something has to do with the time of year. A naturalist has a general idea of seasonal patterns. We notice the appearance and disappearance of the flora and fauna and know, to a degree, the order in which they come and go. For instance, in the Northeast, we won't be expecting to see hummingbirds in January or luna moths in October (which makes it all the more exciting when we do). Every day of the year offers the quarry for a treasure hunt.

June is a month ripe with such possibilities. What came to mind on that early summer morning was a northern spring salamander. At that point, I had yet to actually see one in person. It was one of three New England salamanders that still eluded me. Naturally, the ones that were easiest to find I saw first. With the law of diminishing returns in full effect, coming upon those last three would require more effort. Fortunately, Noble Proctor, a noted Connecticut naturalist, knew of a spot where northern spring salamanders could be located. In fact, Dr. Proctor knows where most plants and animals can be found in our state. You say you are looking for something, and he will not only give you the town to look in, but will tell you what rock to look under or treetop to scan. I wasn't surprised that he knew where to find the salamanders I sought.

Spring salamanders, *Gyrinophilus porphyriticus*, are listed as Threatened in Connecticut. That means that there are no more than nine occurrences in the state, and that they are likely to become endangered in the foreseeable future. That next step, Endangered, means it is in danger of becoming extirpated. Species that are extirpated, or extinct in their range, rarely return.

Spring salamanders, Noble told me, could be found in a stream up in the northern part of the state, right on the border of Massachusetts. The town of Barkhamstead, in addition to harboring these rare salamanders, could also boast hosting the occasional moose that wanders through. Moose in our state are rare, although they seem to be moving in. A Connecticut moose is something I would have to stare at for a long time before I'd believe what I was seeing.

At that time, John Acorn, a naturalist from Alberta, Canada, whom I had booked to speak for the Connecticut Butterfly Association later that night, was staying with me. He, along with Mike DiGiorgio, a wildlife artist, banjo picker, and fellow amphibian enthusiast, joined me.

The dirt road Noble had described was a challenge to find. In fact, we searched along the wrong road for awhile before we realized our mistake. But eventually we did locate the right road, as evidenced by the swift-moving stream that ran alongside it. These spring salamanders were supposed to be in the stream, or more specifically, under rocks along the edge of the stream. We flipped rocks until we uncovered the magnificent creature we sought. While I had seen pictures of the spring salamander before, I was taken aback by its size. At about seven inches long, it was the largest I'd ever seen. It was a beautiful pumpkin orange, almost the color of a red eft, which I think comes pretty close to neon. The spring salamanders have a flattened body, an adaptation that allows them to hug the ground as they navigate the rushing stream. This one sat out in the open, allowing us to take all the pictures we wanted. When the photo session ended, I got greedy and tried to pick it up. It may as well have been an eel. It was remarkably quick and shot through the water and under another rock.

It was a great day—we found what we were looking for. We even had the added bonus of finding an erythristic redback salamander, which was another first for me. These are the same species as the redbacks common throughout the Northeast, but this one was bright orange, similar to the spring salamander. It's believed that this color morph is a form of Batesean mimicry, which gives the appearance of a toxic red-spotted newt.

•

The following June I was ready for another visit with my big orange friends, so I gave Frank Gallo a call. He had not been able to join me the year before, much to my disappointment. Frank can find himself in the most incredible parts of the world, and has done so repeatedly without taking a dime from his own pocket. He pulls it off because he is a fun guy to have along. His enjoyment of birds borders on obsessive, but his enthusiasm sweeps you up, and you find yourself caring more than you would have imagined about finding that rare sparrow in a cornfield or godwit on the beach. In addition, he is good at finding things. Even if he has never been there before, he has a sense of where to go to find whatever you are looking for. He is that good. He also enjoys both listening to and telling stories.

Frank has now parlayed these talents into a career in ecotourism. People who like people tend to be liked by people. This could explain why Frank has a toothbrush in the guest bathroom in innumerable houses across the country.

Two other friends were also up for the trip: Cindi Kobak and Bill Yule. Cindi is a naturalist I had met years ago when we both did wildlife rehabilitation. She is a writer and artist who holds a special fondness for the more underappreciated creatures. Hanging on my refrigerator for the longest time was a picture she took of a rat-tailed maggot. It was a great shot that captured the true essence of the creature. (If you have never seen one, they basically look like fat white maggots with a long ratlike tail, which is actually a breathing apparatus. Betsy didn't think the refrigerator was the best place for the photo. But where else would you hang it? Anyway, it disappeared, and I have my suspicions.)

I wrote a bit about Bill Yule in my previous book, *Discovering Moths*. He is another all-around naturalist with a fascination for all that is wild. While he knows more than most about mushrooms and wildflowers, he has branched off into dragonflies, moths, and

Cindi Kobak BILL KOBAK PHOTO

now rove beetles. For every creature on this earth, there is someone to appreciate it. One of those people is often Bill.

Betsy joined us as well. Of all the different creatures I've gotten into, amphibians seem to be the ones that really grab her interest. She has an amazing knack for finding them, too. It will be no surprise for her to read that I credit her with being able to find things better than I can. She could regale you with tales of my frantic searches for lost shoes, keys, glasses, and channel changers, which she finds within seconds. Luckily, that same talent can be applied outdoors as well. Many of the most interesting finds in my yard, from marbled salamanders to Polyphemus moths, have resulted from her inadvertently coming across them. (She also finds four-leafed clovers better than anyone I know, but then her maiden name *is* Shanahan.)

Barkhamstead is about an hour and a half from my part of the state. Cindi, Bill, Betsy, and I drove together and met Frank at a deli in Barkhamstead. After a quick lunch, our search was on.

You have to flip a lot of rocks to find spring salamanders. They prefer to hang out under the flat rocks along the banks of moving streams. Since they are highly sensitive to pollution, the stream has to be pristine. Moving water is more oxygenated than still water, and an amphibian that breathes through its skin—spring salamanders are lungless—would find this advantageous for gas exchange.

In looking for spring salamanders, I had discovered two things: There is a better chance of finding

Frank Gallo CINDI KOBAK PHOTO

them in the mini coves along the stream edge, and it is best to get yourself wet right away. You waste too much time carefully skipping from rock to rock trying to keep your feet dry. Just walk into the damn water. Let it fill your shoes. Soak yourself up to your knees. Become the stream. Sure it's cold, but once you get it over with, you don't worry about it anymore.

The five of us searched the eastern bank of the stream for about an hour and a half, maybe longer, and were having no luck. We found a few dusky salamanders, a species that actually gets eaten by the much larger spring sallies. We found some crayfish, too, which made me hungry. (I was about a week into the Atkins diet, and just about everything made me think of food.)

Frank had found a good-sized branch to serve as a walking stick. It soon turned into a pointer as he stood uphill from us and indicated rocks for Bill and me to turn. "Flip your own damn rocks!" I shouted up to him. Frank laughed in response.

We moved up the stream and down again, bent at waist and knee, flipping rock after rock after rock. We had driven a good distance to get here, and while I knew everyone understood that no guarantees come with such forays, I was feeling some pressure to find something, or for *someone* to find something. I looked up from my umpteenth rock to see Bill forging across the river. The current was pretty strong, which is what had kept us from trying the other side earlier. Bill had apparently found a more shallow area to cross. Betsy and Cindi were unable, or unwilling, to cross where we did and they continued to search on their side. Betsy took a nice diver off the rocks, which put her in the "we're wet now and don't care anymore" club. Frank was nowhere to be seen.

We continued to work our way downstream, flipping rock after rock. When I had begun this endeavor, I'd expected to find something every time I flipped a rock. I was now at the point where I expected to fail to uncover the elusive salamander. When I finally did find one, its surprise in seeing me was greatly reciprocated.

"Got one!" I shouted.

Bill, who was about fifty feet upriver, soon joined me. He was clearly glad to be seeing this creature for the first time. Betsy and Cindi were trying to find a place to cross the stream.

"Frank, we got one!" I shouted again. There was no answer.

Bill and I looked at the now exposed salamander. We realized that it would not sit there long before looking for cover. Once it worked its way into the submerged rocks, it could be very difficult to find again. Using the surrounding rocks, we began to build a little containment area. The salamander wedged itself as deeply as it could under one of the walls, and we knew it would only be a matter of time before it found some way to get out.

Meanwhile, Betsy and Cindi hadn't found a place to cross and Frank was still missing. That's when Bill suggested we bring the salamander to them.

"I don't know," I said. "I tried to pick one up last time, and it was like trying to hold onto an eel."

"I don't think it's going to be here long enough for the others to see," said Bill.

"Do you think you can catch it?" I asked.

"I think so."

"Go for it."

Bill reached into the water and put his hand over the salamander. My hands hovered over his, as backup. He quickly grabbed the amphibian and lifted it out of the water. I was impressed until it squirmed out of his hand. He caught it with his other hand, but it shot out like a little wriggly missile. That's when I saved the day by grabbing it. A split second later it was free again, and after a few more boggles, the salamander was back in the water, over the wall of our little fortress, and gone for good.

"You got one?" came Frank's voice from behind us.

"Well, sort of," I said.

"Where is it?" he asked.

"It got away."

Frank was not happy, and the excitement Bill and I shared in seeing a spring salamander was dampened by our not being able to share the find with everyone.

We did a little more rock flipping before deciding to call it quits. The spring salamanders just weren't making it easy for us today. I really didn't want to drive back home with nothing to show for our efforts, and I had an idea. There is another amphibian, the slimy salamander, *Plethodon gluti-nosus*, that has been documented in an area about forty or so minutes away. It was a bit out of the way, but we had come this far, so why not?

This species is even more rare than the spring salamander, and I had never seen one. None of us had. A map in Michael Klemens's book, *The Amphibians and Reptiles of Connecticut and the Adjacent Regions*, shows its general location in Fairfield County in western Connecticut. The area is indicated by big red dots, which fall far from pinpointing the exact area in which to look. (Each red dot works out to be several miles in scale.) Two of the dots were in Pootatuck State Forest, a 1,155-acre woodland named for the Mohican word for "river of falls." It would be a long shot, but we were going to give it a try; we found it on our map and were off.

Pootatuck is primarily a mixed deciduous forest, as are most Connecticut state forests. In his book, Klemens noted that specimens were found in mature forest in areas where a lot of duff was present. Unlike the *porphyriticus*, the slimys would be found under rotten logs on land, so we went from flipping rocks to flipping logs. In doing so we turned up the occasional red-spotted newt, redback salamander, and a spotted salamander. All were fun to uncover, especially the spotted, all big and shiny, which we hadn't expected to see. I wasn't optimistic about finding a slimy salamander, but we had nothing to lose.

Darkness was approaching, and we had already flipped about a hundred rotten logs. I was hungry, and our whining was beginning to escalate. Then, from about a hundred feet away, I heard "Bingo!" We ran over to where Betsy stood, holding something cupped in her hands. She opened them to reveal what looked like a young Jefferson salamander. It was partially covered in debris from the ground and was jet black speckled with

Bingo! A juvenile slimy salamander!

Spotted Salamander Life Cycle

Spotted salamander spermatophores

A spotted salamander larva,
the lion of the pond

An egg mass

Spotted Salamander Life Cycle

A larva toward the end of development (note the tail—nipped by another salamander)

A juvenile spotted salamander

An adult spotted salamander

Wood Frog Life Cycle

A wood frog egg mass

Newly hatched tadpoles feed on algae growing on the egg mass.

Wood Frog Life Cycle

A tadpole growing legs

A froglet on a lily pad

An adult wood frog

Mole Salamanders

Spotted salamander

Marbled salamander (female)

Marbled salamander (male)

Marbled salamander larva

Mole Salamanders

Jefferson salamander FRANK GALLO

A Jefferson salamander hybrid (*laterale jeffersonianum jeffersonianum*)

A blue-spotted salamander hybrid (*laterale laterale jeffersonianum*)

Juvenile blue-spotted salamander

Lungless Salamanders

Allegheny mountain dusky salamander SOLON MORSE

Northern two-lined salamander

Two-lined salamander larva

A two-lined salamander egg mass
just prior to hatching

Northern Dusky salamander

A juvenile dusky blending in with the muddy bank

Four-toed salamander

Lungless Salamanders

Black flecks on an ivory background mark the four-toed salamander's belly.

Northern redback salamander

The lead-back salamander is gray form of the redback.

Erythristic redback salamander

JOHN ACORN PHOTO

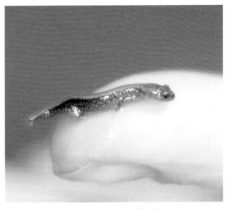

A newly emerged redback

In profile, the spring salamander shows a square snout.

Northern spring salamander

Lungless Salamanders

A Northern slimy salamander close-up

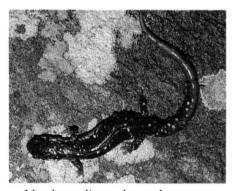

Northern slimy salamander

A juvenile slimy salamander

Eastern hellbender

R.G. SPRACKLAND,
VIRTUAL MUSEUM OF
NATURAL HISTORY

Newts

A gravid (pregnant) red-spotted newt

Red-spotted newt in intermediate form, transforming into adult

Red eft

Mudpuppiess

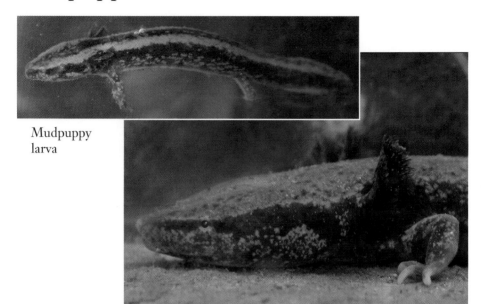

Mudpuppy
larva

Northern mudpuppy

A mudpuppy
head-on

A juvenile mudpuppy

Spadefoot Toads

Eastern spadefoot toad TOM TYNING PHOTO

A swimming spadefoot TOM TYNING PHOTO

True Toads

A sub-adult American toad

American toad

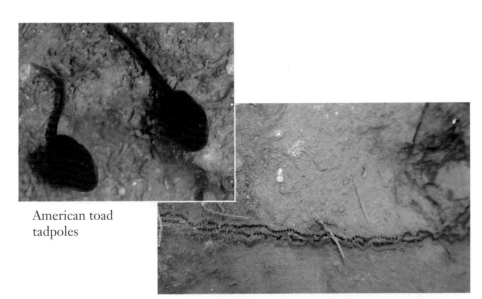

American toad
tadpoles

Egg strings from an American toad

An American toadlet

True Toads

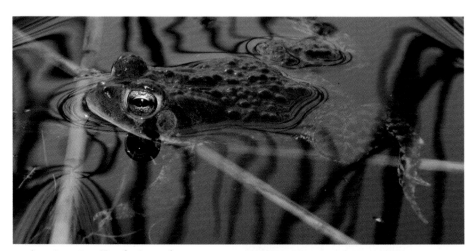

A swimming Fowler's toad

A Fowler's toad calling

A Fowler's toadlet

A Fowler's toad with lighter base color

Hylidae

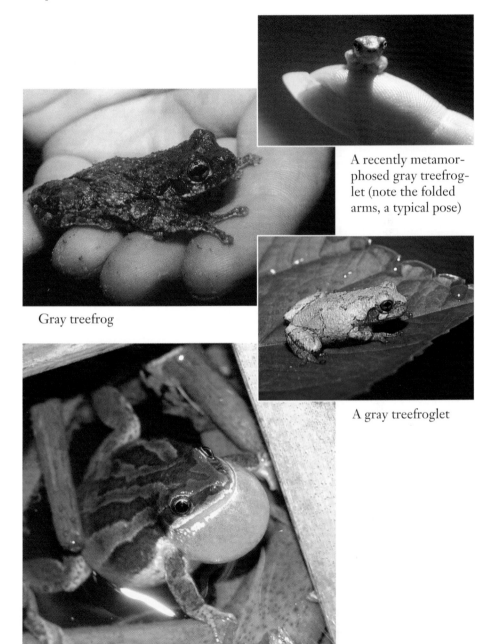

A recently metamor-
phosed gray treefrog-
let (note the folded
arms, a typical pose)

Gray treefrog

A gray treefroglet

Western chorus frog SOLON MORSE

Hylidae

The characteristic X pattern on a spring peeper's back

A spring peeper calling

Spring peeper tadpole

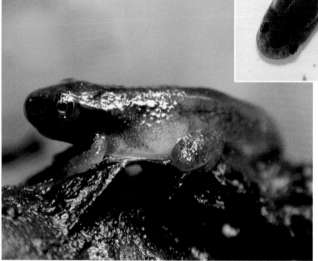

A newly metamorphosed peeper

True Frogs

Bullfrog (male)

Bullfrog (female)

A bullfrog tadpole

A juvenile bullfrog

True Frogs

Green frog

A juvenile green frog

Mink frog
TOM TYNING PHOTO

A pickerel frog tadpole

A juvenile pickerel frog

A pickerel frog on ice

True Frogs

A developing leopard frog

A leopard frog tadpole

Northern leopard frog

Wood frog

white dots. Having studied the photo and read the description of this sala-mander in Klemens' book, I wondered if this was indeed a slimy. Slimys are supposed to be huge by New England salamander standards—up to seven or so inches long. This little guy was just a couple inches from nose to tail, but the tail was rounded, not keeled as in a Jefferson, and the dots were more defined. We determined that what Betsy held was a juvenile slimy salamander.

She did it. She found the rarest salamander in Connecticut.

We had worked hard for this find, and elation was in the air. With only twelve species of salamanders in New England, finding a new one was very special for us. It was such an uplifting moment that I will always be able to replay it in my mind.

We took turns photographing it, and then Cindi suggested we get an underside photo of it, too. This was a very good idea; the dark venter helped nail its identification as a slimy when I read the full description later. We returned the slimy little fellow back to where Betsy had found it, and gently replaced the log.

Driving home in the dark, I couldn't help get out of my mind that as thrilling as it was to find a new species, it would have been even better to see an adult.

June 20th, Father's Day, which is my day. I get to do whatever I want on this day, and my family has to do it with me—it's in the contract. Betsy has the same deal for Mother's Day, which usually leads to a nice spring drive to some out-of-the-way nursery or garden center. Or she puts us to work in the yard. In fact, on the Mother's Day preceding my big day, she had us plant about two hundred pine and spruce seedlings she had ordered. (Okay, *we* had ordered.)

On this particular Father's Day, when Betsy asked me what I wanted to do, I told her, "I want to go back and see if we can find an adult slimy salamander." This would teach her to put us to work on Mother's Day. But she was up for it, and so was my daughter Lizzie.

So, there we were, hot and sticky in a mosquito-infested forest, rolling over log after log. We rolled a lot of them—about a hundred or so. As luck would have it, I came to the very same log Betsy had flipped a couple of weeks earlier to discover that young slimy salamander. This log was special to me. It was an amphibian shrine, if you will. It lay at the base of a small, damp berm and was about three and a half feet long, a foot in diameter, and spongy with wood rot. I gave the log a roll. Looking up at me were the eyes of a huge salamander—a seven-and-a-half-inch-long, full adult slimy salamander. There was no questioning this one. As with the juvenile, its body was black, but the spots were far greater in number and in some places joined together to form white blotches. This was a very aware creature, too; it lifted its head to assess its status after the sudden loss of cover.

As was now the tradition, I shouted, "Bingo!" and was soon joined by my wife and daughter. There was no sign of the juvenile that we had seen on our previous trip, which meant one of three things: This adult had eaten it; the juveniles grow at an amazing rate; or there was something about that log that slimy salamanders find attractive. I'm leaning strongly toward the last hunch.

I took a whole bunch of pictures, which is my way of celebrating a good find, and thanked the salamander for being where I happened to look. I then returned the log to the position it had been prior to my disturbing it. This was, without a doubt, the most memorable Father's Day for me, and I believe I can safely say Betsy and Lizzie were as thrilled as I was. In fact, Betsy must have really enjoyed it, because the next Mother's Day was spent taking a nice spring drive in the country.

•

It's June again, and it's two years later. The phone rings. Frank wants to try and find that spring salamander again. Let's hope three's a charm.

7

Canaries in the Coal Mine

ON AN OVERCAST morning on August 8, 1995, eight middle school students from the Minnesota New Country School gathered for a hike. They were part of a nature study class taught by Cindy Reinitz, and their destination was Ney Woods, a six-hundred-acre farm owned by Donald Ney, who welcomed people to explore his property.

Arriving at the farm, the kids spilled out of the van. As they walked to the fields, they saw young Northern leopard frogs hopping about. The children caught a few and realized that these were not normal frogs. Their legs were missing, or in some cases, they had too many legs. At first, they attributed these oddities to injuries sustained while being caught, but in short time, they realized something was wrong. They headed down to the pond and discovered more of the same. Of the twenty-two frogs they caught that morning, eleven were malformed.

The students collected data on these frogs, filling their books with notes and drawings. They posted photos of three of the frogs on the Internet, hoping that someone out there could tell them what caused these abnormalities. In the meantime, Cindy Reinitz made some phone calls, including one to Dr. Judy Helgen, a research biologist in the Minnesota Pollution Control Agency's water-quality division. It so happened that Dr. Helgen had followed up on a report of similarly malformed frogs in Granite Falls two years earlier. That report had gone nowhere, maybe due to the fact that, the following spring, most of the frogs in that area appeared normal. But now Dr. Helgen knew of two sites showing the same phenomenon.

Dr. Helgen got more of her colleagues involved, and in no time at all, the story of these deformed frogs was on TV, radio, and the Associated Press newswire, making celebrities of the children. All across the county, people began checking the frogs in their own ponds, and many found malformed specimens. Today, frogs with missing, malformed, or extra limbs, facial malformations, and internal aberrations—have been documented in forty-four states and also in Japan, Canada, and several countries in

Europe. Sixty species are known to have been affected, and in some populations, up to 60 percent of the amphibians exhibit malformations. While spotty records of deformed frogs have existed since the 1700s, it appears the problem has been increasing rapidly.

•

Nothing is more vulnerable to its environment than an amphibian. It starts with the egg, which over time evolved to contend with natural predators, seasonal changes, and other elements threatening to thwart its development. However, because it lacks a protective shell, it is open to relatively new threats, such as chemical changes in the water and ultraviolet light from above. Within the egg, the first embryonic cell division takes place, and everything has to go just so; the slightest deviation can wreak havoc on the amphibian anatomy.

If the egg hatches, the tadpole is susceptible to the same modern-day environmental threats as the egg—more pollutants added to the body, more radiation from above. In species that spend more time in the water in a larval stage, such as green frogs and bullfrogs, the exposure to contaminants increases, increasing, too, the potential for malformations in those species.

Then, the adult amphibian, upon absorbing its gills, is given the most remarkable covering—skin that breathes. This permeable skin is designed to efficiently exchange gases and water. The catch is that the amphibian must keep its skin from drying out, forcing it to remain in frequent contact with water. If that water is anything but pure, the accumulation of toxins taken in through the skin can cause a myriad of problems for that frog. Because they are so intimate with their surroundings, amphibians are affected before any of us can see trouble a-brewing. They are the canaries in the coal mine.

So naturally the question is, What is causing these malformations? You may have noticed that I use the word *malformation* instead of the more commonly used term, *deformation*. "Deformed frogs" was the original description of this phenomenon, but it proved to be inaccurate. A deformation occurs when an existing body part is disfigured. A malformation is the disruption of a body part during development. X-rays of these frogs show that these aberrations are not injuries. Something is causing the frogs to grow wrong.

Within a year of the original discovery of malformed frogs, government agencies went to work to figure out what was happening. Because many people across the country were now diving into this puzzle, it was agreed that one entity should collect all the data. The North American Reporting Center for Amphibian Malformations was established at the Northern Prairie Wildlife Research Center in Jamestown, North Dakota. They are charged with standardizing the data collected by universities and federal and state research groups.

At this writing, it's been ten years since the major thrust of that research began. We still are not completely sure what is causing all these abnormalities. What can be generally agreed upon is that no single catalyst exists, and the phenomenon is the result of a combination of factors. Right now, three possible causes are garnering the most attention: contaminants in the water, increased ultraviolet radiation, and parasites.

•

All kinds of things get into water—metals, herbicides, petroleum products, and fertilizers, to name a few. They get washed down land and collect in the lowest areas on a plain. That's where the water is. That's also where the frogs and salamanders are. Many of the sites in which malformed frogs have been found are near agricultural fields that are heavily sprayed with herbicides and pesticides. Some scientists believe that those chemicals, acting alone or in combination with other agents, such as increased ultraviolet light, could have something to do with the abnormalities.

Endocrine disrupters, in the form of natural and manmade chemicals, are high on the list of suspects. These compounds interfere with the hormones that control development. No one knows for sure how many of these chemicals are out there. Retinoids are being looked at more closely because they have been shown to induce frog malformations in the laboratory. They have also been found in ponds where these malformations have occurred. Retinoids are a class of molecules that includes Vitamin A and retinoic acid, a potent hormone. These are the ingredients you find in the acne medication Accutane. It is legally required that any female going on Accutane get a pregnancy test first because the medicine is known to cause birth defects in all vertebrates.

At least one pesticide out there acts like a retinoid—methoprene. This is a larvicide that prevents insects from reaching sexual maturity. It is often used in mosquito control and is broadcast over wide areas. While the Environmental Protection Agency (EPA) considers it nontoxic to humans, there is a concern over what happens as the compounds break down after exposure to sunlight because retinoids are formed during that process.

According to Dr. David Gardiner, a research biologist at the University of California, retinoids are the cause of frog mutations. He believes that the peculiar kinds of limb deformities seen in amphibians mimic the symptoms of exposure to this compound. However, according to studies led by Stanley K. Sessions at Hartwick College in Oneonta, New York, the mutations found in some frogs are not always consistent with the effects of retinoids. While this compound has been proven to halt limb growth and cause growth of duplicate appendages when applied to the developing leg bud of a tadpole, some of the limb growths observed in the wild are different from what can be achieved in the lab.

It has been known for decades that certain endocrine-disrupting chemicals affect reproduction in wildlife. It is also known that aquatic carnivores are hit hardest because they are at the top of the food chain, where high levels of persistent chemicals build up over time. It is believed that chemicals such as PCBs, dioxin, and selenium (used for copy machines and making glass) are responsible for weakening the eggshells of birds of prey, causing crossed bills in fish-eating birds, and reducing the populations of seals, fish, and alligators.

Dr. Martin Ouellet left his veterinary practice to spend more time tracking down the reason for all the amphibian deformities along the Saint Lawrence River Valley in Montreal. He and a team of Canadian Wildlife biologists examined about thirty thousand frogs, as well as seven species of salamanders. They have catalogued twenty-five types of malformations among the sixteen species of amphibians. Their autopsies have shown what was going on inside the frogs to be just as chilling as a leg growing from a belly or an eyeball in the middle of a back. Livers were yellow and clogged, DNA was altered, and frogs that appeared to be male were female. Ouellet's research shows that in agricultural areas where chemicals and pesticides are used regularly, an average of twenty percent of the amphibians showed limb malformations. In nonagricultural areas, the occurrence is about 1.5 in every hundred. On one farm, every single frog he found was malformed. It got to the point where if they saw a pond by a farm field, Ouellet's team fully expected it to be filled with malformed amphibians; they were proved right over and over again.

Another thing the researchers noticed is that all the altered individuals were juveniles, which means that these afflicted frogs don't live long, which only adds to the concern that this phenomenon is accelerating the rate of amphibian decline.

There is concern, too, that whatever is causing malformations in these aquatic animals may also be affecting humans. A 1996 study performed by researchers at the University of Minnesota showed an increased occurrence of chromosomal aberrations in the children of men who applied pesticides to farms. In addition, children who were conceived in the spring, the busy season for pesticide appliers in western Minnesota, exhibited a higher level of these abnormalities. Additional research in the United States, Canada, and Finland has found that mothers who work in agricultural industries have higher incidences of miscarriage and stillborn children. Children of parents who work or live in these settings have more malformations such as missing or fused fingers and toes, malformed limbs, and abnormal kidneys, hearts, and sexual organs.

What is not known is the exact effect of these chemicals on cell growth. We have many leads, and maybe even a smoking gun, but there is more to the puzzle.

•

Over the past twenty-five or so years, scientists have observed an increasingly large opening in the sky and a general thinning in the ozone layer. Since this discovery, measurements show a three percent decrease of this gas across the globe. Apparently, what we need to do is either develop a really big ozone plug, or just stop making the hole bigger. Of course some are not concerned with the breaking down of this atmosphere—hell, it still looks the same up there—but there is little question that this compromised integrity of our ozone barrier is letting more ultraviolet light slip through to the planet. And no one can say that that's a good thing.

Consequently, many of us are more careful to put on sunscreen before we go outside. Ultraviolet, or UV, light is known to cause skin cancer. It may also cause problems for frogs. In 1997, researchers at the Environmental Protection Agency in Duluth, Minnesota, put this to the test with Northern leopard frogs. First, they introduced the insecticide methoprene to a controlled environment in varying amounts. (Remember, this is the compound that could have the potential for disrupting endocrine process in developing animals.) Some of the frogs were then also dosed with UV light during their embryonic and tadpole stages. The UV level was meant to mimic what would be occurring in the spring outdoors in that part of the world. The other frogs were shielded from the UV rays.

Both groups exposed to the highest doses of methoprene showed a high rate of malformations, whether they were under the UV light or not. At all levels of methoprene, however, including the very lowest, the frogs put under the UV light showed a fifty percent increased incidence of malformations. While the researchers could not replicate natural conditions one hundred percent, the research did show that it could be worthwhile to pursue this avenue further.

Scientists know that UV radiation causes the formation of cyclobutane pyrimidine dimers. These are cell poisoning, mutagenic products of DNA. Because the eggs of frogs are clear or translucent, the radiation zaps the embryos while the cells are forming and falling into place. Shallow water provides little shelter from UV radiation, although areas shaded from the sun do tend to offer some protection. It would be interesting to note whether there is a difference between the spotted salamanders that emerge from cloudy eggs and others that develop in clear eggs. Both can often be found side by side in a pond. If the UV radiation continues to increase, we may someday find only clouded egg masses in the vernal pools because the clear ones will have long since been mutated out of existence.

As with pollution, UV radiation as an explanation for amphibian malformations is still a theory. It may affect the animals directly or even, as some suggest, act as an agent to change harmless compounds into something more toxic. It is relatively safe to assume that the two potential causes, pollution and UV light, could be working together, one weakening the frog while the other has its way with it.

Joseph Kiesecker, professor of biology at Penn State, has found strong evidence of another environmental one-two punch that harms amphibian populations. For ten years, he and his team of researchers backpacked into Oregon's Cascades, where the Western toads breed and lay hundreds of thousands of eggs in huge communal masses. Kiesecker and his team used boxes to anchor the eggs at different levels in the water, thus exposing them to different levels of UV light. What they found was that the toads hatched at the shallower depths were too weak to stave off a water mold pathogen called *Saprolegnia ferax*. Nearly all of them died. The toads coming from the deeper levels were not weakened by the UV radiation and were unaffected by the mold.

Kiesecker had set out to find a link between global warming and declines in local amphibian populations. He had observed a direct link between fluctuating temperatures in the South Pacific (Southern Oscillation Index) and the amount of rain or snow in the Cascade Mountains. When El Niño and other meteorological factors cause less precipitation in the Cascades, the shallower water left the amphibians more vulnerable to pathogens. He summarized an even more sobering conclusion in a Penn State publication:

> There is a very strong link between water depth and embryonic mortality. Then there is a link between the Southern Oscillation Index and rainfall patterns in the Cascades. Next there is a link between rainfall patterns and depth at which embryos develop. And finally there is a link between egg-laying depth and mortality associated with *Saprolegnia ferax*.

He goes on to say that "Stress-related disease is the one consistent factor that may link amphibian deaths worldwide, and we have demonstrated that amphibian stress in the Cascades is ultimately linked to recent global climate fluctuations."

Based on this and other studies, it seems that while ozone depletion and consequent higher UV radiation exposure can play a role in weakening its victims, the knockout punch comes from elsewhere. In the last couple decades we've lost three percent of our ozone. What happens if it gets to six percent or ten percent? Right now, increased UV levels could be mutating, and killing, amphibians all over the planet at an alarming rate. They're also being blamed for increased rates of skin cancer and glaucoma in humans. If we can figure out what's causing these amphibian malformations and this global die-off, we humans will most likely benefit. If there are so many contaminants in the water that it's brewing up twelve-legged frogs, then maybe that's telling us something about the water we humans *also* rely on to stay alive. If the sun is baking frog embryos into three-eyed curiosities, that may be telling us that we need to do something to keep that protective ozone blanket above us.

●

A third culprit is also being blamed for frog malformations—parasites. About ten years before the discovery of malformed frogs on that middle school outing, herpetologist Stephen Ruth came upon a site in California where hundreds of long-toed salamanders and Pacific treefrogs were exhibiting a wide array of abnormalities. He contacted colleague Stanley K. Sessions, who first suspected chemicals in the water. However, water samples tested clean. What they discovered instead were cysts in the malformed amphibians. The cysts were from parasitic trematodes, which are also known as flatworms or flukes. About forty known species of trematodes are considered to be parasites. The ones found by Sessions are in the genus *Ribeiroia*, and while unnamed at the time of their discovery, are now called *Ribeiroia ondatrae*.

Ribeiroia trematodes enter a water body in their adult stage via droppings from birds, most typically herons, raptors, and ducks. They lay eggs in their new habitat, and the eggs hatch into miracidia, a larval stage that enters mollusks, such as pond snails, to continue their development. They change form again, into cercariae, grow a little squiggly tail, and find their next host, a frog or salamander larva. There, they burrow into the skin, sometimes right where the leg buds are forming, and form metacercarial cysts. Birds then eat the amphibians, and the cycle continues.

Closer study of the California frogs and salamanders revealed high concentrations of tiny round cysts at the base of leg joints. Sessions believed that their presence caused the leg buds to grow abnormally. He tested his hypothesis by placing glass beads, the size of trematode cysts, in the leg buds of developing frogs and salamanders. This resulted in frogs with malformed or extra limbs. The manner of the deformities mirrored what was being observed in the wild. Sessions concluded:

> It has been experimentally demonstrated that trematode cyst infestation can cause the complete range of limb deformities that have been observed in field-caught amphibians. These deformities include asymmetrical combinations of whole extra limbs, mirror image duplications, bony triangles, truncations, and skin fusions. This was shown using an identified parasite that is abundantly found at confirmed deformed frog sites, and using the infectious larval stages (cercariae) at concentrations determined from observed infestation levels in field-caught specimens.

Scientists believe they have an understanding of the process. This form of reproduction gives the trematodes an evolutionary advantage at the expense of their amphibian hosts. Most parasites do not kill their hosts; once a host is dead, the parasite's food source is gone and its chances of getting from one place to another are diminished. However, a trematode that cripples its frog host benefits because that frog is an easier catch for a predatory bird, the next crucial vector in the parasite's life cycle. The cysts from the eaten frog develop into adult trematodes within the bird and are then deposited in a new habitat.

The problem today is that these parasites seem to be establishing themselves in more and more habitats.

Pieter Johnson, a doctoral student at the Center for Limnology,

University of Wisconsin, was aware of Sessions's work and conducted some experiments of his own. He, with Kevin Lunde and Euan Ritchie, exposed laboratory-raised tadpoles of Pacific treefrogs to different numbers of *Ribeiroia cercariae*. Some got none; some got up to forty-eight. The cyst-free tadpoles developed normally. The unlucky ones subjected to the parasites either died or developed into severely malformed treefrogs. The malformations occuring in lab-raised frogs were in line with those observed in the field.

Johnson and other partners expanded their research to encompass more of California and parts of Oregon, Washington, Idaho, and Montana. They compared the level of malformations with concentrations of pesticides and trematode populations. They found that the presence of the parasites was a strong predictor of amphibian malformation, while pesticides did not seem to be a factor. In fact, a presence of high numbers of ramshorn snails (*Planorbella tenuis*), the aquatic snail acting as one of the tag team hosts of *Ribeiroia*, predicted a population of amphibians with a high percentage of deformities, and vice versa.

Studies of frogs throughout the rest of the country have continued to show a connection between amphibian aberrations and *Ribeiroia* trematodes. In fact, that connection was also confirmed in the pond of malformed frogs discovered by Cindy Reinitz's students. Lab tests on many of the species subjected to this phenomenon also consistently show them to be hosts to the crippling trematodes.

•

But why now? Why are we witnessing a virtual explosion of frogs being mutated by trematodes? One explanation has to be that a lot more people are out there looking for them. An example of how this can work occurred in Connecticut. In the early 1990s, a butterfly known as Leonard's skipper, was listed as extirpated from that state. Then, a population showed up in the town of Hamden. Shortly after that, the Connecticut Butterfly Association was formed, connecting hundreds of people interested in butterflies. With all those extra eyes now looking for these insects, Leonard's skippers were found in several other places. So were two other extirpated species. Frog malformations have been a hot topic for over a decade now, and what was once just a few herpetologists poking around for this oddity is now a huge national and multinational effort. You know who finds a lot of them? Kids. Not necessarily kids looking for mutated frogs, but just kids chasing frogs.

That's not the whole reason, though. I wish it were, but some attention has to be paid to the primary incubator of this epidemic—the pond snails. When a trematode larva enters a snail, it multiples. One larva becomes many hundreds of larvae. An increase of just twenty snails in a habitat could add up to twenty thousand flatworms. This could have a dramatic effect on the amphibian population, especially if it is already weakened by other factors.

An explosion in parasite-hosting snail populations could have varying effects on the frogs and salamanders. One large factor would involve timing. Where and when the cercariae enter the tadpole would dictate the level of interference. On the most extreme side, the highest level of interference would be death. On the lower end of the scale, there could be little or no visible evidence. This could be part of the reason why amphibian populations can have good years and bad years.

The other reason may have to do with us. Snails eat algae, and fertilizer makes algae grow fast. Fertilizer comes in many forms—spray, powder, and manure. As rainwater percolates through the soil, it picks up fertilizer residue and carries it to its final destination. This nitrogen-loaded fertilizer, being fertilizer, makes green plants grow, and one of the fastest growing green aquatic plants is algae. Johnson and Andrew Blausten wrote about this connection in a 2003 *Scientific American* article:

> We recently showed a direct relation between human habitat alteration and sites where *Ribeiroia* parasites are especially abundant. Indeed, our survey of the western US, reported in 2002, revealed that 44 of the 59 wetlands in which amphibians were infected by *Ribeiroia* were reservoirs, farm ponds, or other artificial bodies of water. Fertilizer runoff and cattle manure near these habitats often encourage overwhelming blooms of algae, which means more food for the snails that host *Ribeiroia* parasites. Larger populations of snails infected with *Ribeiroia* lead directly to more deformed frogs. Wading birds, the other necessary parasite hosts, are usually found in abundance at such human-made locales.

And again, if the trematodes don't already exist in some form within a pond, the timing of their introduction to the habitat will be as critical as the timing of their emergence from the snails. Based on the increasing frequency of malformation reports, it certainly does appear that all the circumstances have been falling together in the trematodes' favor with more and more frequency.

It should be mentioned that research has been conducted to determine whether the frogs themselves are responsible for the malformations. It appears that sometimes they are. Some populations will host a number of cannibalistic individuals. In an attempt to devour their brethren, frogs and tadpoles have been known to nibble off a leg bud or a newly formed limb. This would cause either missing limbs or deformed limbs upon regeneration. I have witnessed this in both frog and salamander populations. In every instance, there seemed to be an overabundance of the young amphibians in relation to the size of their habitat. Many of them were missing chunks of tail, limbs, and in a couple individuals, an eye.

I am sure this accounts for some of the malformations, but probably not all. Amphibians have been nipping at each other as long as there have been amphibians. That may even be part of the reason they evolved the ability to regenerate appendages. Unless something has really been ticking them off in the last decade, an increase in this behavior would be unlikely.

●

Another bizarre phenomenon has recently cropped up in the Altona district of Hamburg, Germany. Toads are exploding. The toads appear to be normal, and then all of a sudden they inflate to three and a half times their normal size and explode, sending their entrails flying up to three feet in all directions. Biologists are not sure why this is happening. They checked the ponds for contaminants and found none, or at least nothing obvious. Possible suspects are some unknown virus or fungus—or crows. The crows in that area have become adept at removing the livers from these amphibians. They have learned that a few well-placed pecks between the toad's chest and abdominal cavity will provide access to the liver, an avian delicacy. The amphibians puff up in defense, but because they now have a hole in their body, the blood vessels and lungs explode. Whatever the reason, people are being warned to stay away from what has been now dubbed *Tümpel des Todes*, or Pool of Death.

While exploding toads do not fall under the category of malformed frogs, it still has that creepy, science fiction air to it. It's the kind of thing that can really hijack the public's imagination. By contrast, I can't help but marvel at the good science that has been taking place in the area of amphibian malformations. We have somehow managed to steer clear of the crop circle and cow anus–stealing aliens factions. It took a few years, but we are seeing scientists from several fields collaborate to piece this puzzle together, and much of the data collected comes from volunteers throughout the country. Naturally, the researchers have been led down some dead-end paths, but that's part of the process. The proponents for the three suggested causes of the malformations generally agree that there could be connections between them, although there are still stubborn (and maybe rightfully so) adherents in each group who claim theirs is the primary cause. My own personal belief as a layman is that the trematodes are the direct cause in the majority of cases, with pollution and UV radiation being indirect causes. Hungry fish and cannibalistic amphibians must also be factored into the picture in some populations.

The research is ongoing, and the more people contributing to it, the better we can perceive the scope of the problem. For one thing, we need to know how long this really has been happening at this level: Are we indeed witnessing a spike in occurrences, or are we simply finding more instances because more of us are looking? Research into the history of this phenomenon suggests we are witnessing a spike. In addition to seeking out causes for the problem, we need to start thinking about solutions. Some have suggested that it could be as simple as dealing with the snails that host the trematodes. Get rid of them, and you break the parasites' cycle.

If you come across a population of malformed amphibians, contact the North American Reporting Center for Amphibian Malformations (NARCAM) either through their Web site at www.npwrc.usgs.gov/narcam or by phone at 800-238-9801.

❧ 8 ❧

Species Accounts

MOLE SALAMANDERS
(Ambystomatidae)

The word *mole* reflects the subterranean nature of this group. Most of their adult life is spent beneath the leaf litter and in underground burrows. Their bodies and limbs could be described as robust. They have five toes on each hind foot and four on the front feet. Their blunt heads lack the naso-labial groove between the nostril and upper lip, a characteristic found in the Plethodontidae, or lungless salamanders.

Marbled salamander,
Ambystoma opacum

About thirty species are contained in this family, all of them found only in North America. New England is home to four species, described below.

A fifth species, the Eastern tiger salamander (*Ambystoma tigrinum*), also deserves mention because its range just barely extends into New York state, where it is listed as Endangered. These salamanders are confined to fewer than one hundred breeding pools in Nassau and Suffolk counties on Long Island. Their name comes from the yellow markings across their dark bodies, and they are among the largest terrestrial salamanders on our continent.

Spotted Salamander
(*Ambystoma maculatum*)

With their bright yellow spots glowing on a deep slate-gray background, the spotted salamander is hard to confuse with other mole salamanders. Come late winter/early spring, spotteds emerge from their overwintering burrows beneath the leaf litter to converge in vernal pools. Here they mate, spend a few days in the water, and head back to the woods.

After the first few warm rainy nights from late March to mid-April, a walk along the edges of a vernal pool may turn up spermatophores and egg masses. The latter are gelatinous structures containing between one hundred and two hundred eggs. A female will lay up to four egg masses in a pool, and they can be either transparent or milky white. Many become infused with algae, which give them a greenish hue. Within four to six weeks, the salamander larvae will wriggle out and begin to feed on a variety of tiny creatures in the pond. They are yellow-brown in color. Tendrilled gills fan out from behind their heads, giving them the appearance of little lions—a suitable look for what will become an upper food chain predator in its habitat. As time goes on, their front legs, and then back legs, appear. Because they utilize vernal pools, they must develop quickly and leave before the water is absorbed by the roots of the surrounding trees.

Once on land, the young salamanders linger around the dried pool for a few weeks, sheltering beneath logs, rocks, and leaves. While they can secrete a sticky, milky substance from their skin to deter predation by mammals, their main defense lies in staying under cover.

These salamanders can live for more than ten years. There are reports of some making it to twenty. They are widespread and common throughout the East.

Marbled Salamander
(*Ambystoma opacum*)

On October 2, 2003, an article appeared in the *Hartford Courant* entitled "A Hurricane's Unusual Gift." It told of an amphibian egg mass appearing on a Connecticut homeowner's porch, compliments of Hurricane Isabel. Local scientists assumed the eggs were carried from as far away as North Carolina, since "No frogs in Connecticut lay eggs this late in the year." They were right about that. However, what they failed to consider was a particular *salamander* that lays eggs in the latter part of the year—the marbled salamander. The egg mass most likely was picked up from a nearby vernal pool and deposited on the person's porch. While this would make for an interesting story in itself, it is not quite as spectacular an image as eggs soaring hundreds of miles through the air.

Autumn is the season for marbled salamanders to shine. While most amphibians breed in the spring and summer months, these amphibians put it off until later in the season. As its common name would suggest, the male is a deeply marbled black and white. The female's body is also black and white, but less solidly patterned. The Latin word *opacum* translates to dark, or obscured. They do blend in quite nicely with the damp, leafy habitats they call home. They are voracious solitary hunters, feeding on a variety of insects, worms, and terrestrial mollusks (slugs and snails). While not as common as spotted salamanders, marbled salamanders can be found with some looking, but most often by chance while gardening or flipping rocks and logs.

After mating, the marbled females lay their eggs in dried-out vernal pools. The salamander wraps her body around the small mass to hold in the moisture and protect the eggs from small predators. Egg laying usually takes place about halfway up the basin of the empty pool. There is a reason for this. Once the eggs become submerged in the rising water of the autumnal rains, they hatch. Had the eggs been laid on the bottom, they could hatch after the first or second good rain, only to become stranded once the water recedes. Positioning the eggs farther up the basin allows the water to reach a more sustainable level for the larvae. If the rains do not fill the pool in autumn, the eggs (fifty to one hundred in a mass) can overwinter and hatch the following spring.

The larvae are similar to those of the spotted salamanders, but generally appear a bit darker as the result of the heavy mottling. Hatching later in the season provides them with the advantage of being one of the few predators within the winter pools. It also reduces the threat of the pool drying out before they are ready to leave. A winter search is sometimes rewarded with the sight of marbled salamander larvae swimming beneath the ice.

Marbled salamanders find their extreme northern limit is just over the southern border of New Hampshire, where they are listed as Endangered. They are listed as Threatened in Massachusetts.

Jefferson Salamander
(*Ambystoma jeffersonianum*)

Jefferson salamanders have much in common with the more frequently encountered spotted salamanders. They both emerge from their underground burrows in late winter/early spring (although Jeffersons usually emerge before spotteds); they are ample-sized mole salamanders (although Jeffersons are a bit smaller); and they are both dependent on vernal pools to reproduce. Their sausage-shaped egg masses are usually attached to twigs and take between a month and a month and a half to hatch. The egg masses are smaller than those of the spotted salamanders, and contain between ten and seventy-five eggs. One female will lay several masses, which, like those of the spotteds, can become infused with algae.

However, Mr. Jefferson's namesakes have even more in common with another Ambystomid, the blue-spotted salamander, with which they interbreed. It can be difficult to distinguish pure Jeffersons from the hybrids, and it often takes a DNA sample to make that call. Any Jefferson or blue-spotted salamander found in southern New England can be suspected of being a hybrid.

That said, there are differences in appearance between the two pure populations, most notably in the blue speckling along the sides. In the Jefferson, the speckling, if it exists at all, is typically more fine—an airbrushed wash of pale gray-blue. More often, the salamander is just a chocolate brown, with very little blue on the sides. In the blue-spotted, the spots are large and distinct. Unfortunately, there are variations in between; in which case, the best the layperson can do is assume it is a hybrid within the Jefferson/blue-spotted complex.

One clue that can be used to help figure out whether or not you have a Jefferson or a blue-spotted is location of the salamander. Breeding Jeffersons utilize fish-free vernal pools, while blue-spotteds will breed in larger bodies of water, including red maple swamps, which are habitats that are not necessarily fish-free. But this should just be a clue, since blue-spotteds will also use vernal pools, and Jeffersons will use swamps if that is all that is available in the area. You can also check the vent, which tends to be surrounded by gray in Jeffersons and black in blue-spotteds.

Lastly, the Jeffersons are more restricted in range. They occur in New York, Connecticut, Massachusetts, New Hampshire, and Vermont, but only west of the Connecticut River. The blue-spotteds are found throughout the Northeast. So, in general, if a hybrid is found east of the Connecticut River, you can call it a blue-spotted. If it is found west of the river, you can call it a Jefferson.

Ambystoma jeffersonianum are listed as a species of Special Concern in Connecticut, Massachusetts, and Vermont.

Blue-spotted Salamander
(*Ambystoma laterale*)

Late winter/early spring rainy nights are the best time to find this attractive, medium-sized, blue-flecked salamander. The species name is meant to draw one's attention to the lateral section, or sides, of the salamander, which, in addition to the dorsal area of the head and tail, are covered with large blue spots. Those spots give them an appearance that has often been compared to old enamel cookware.

As with their larger cousins, the blue-spotteds emerge from their burrows beneath the leaf litter to meet up and mate in a nearby body of water. But, unlike the spotteds and Jeffersons, they are not limited to vernal pools and will breed in permanent swamps where fish may be present. However, if vernal pools are the only habitat available, *laterale*s in the area will be dependent on them. They lay their eggs singly, in small masses of a couple dozen eggs, or in sheets on the pond's bottom. These hatch within a month's time, and the hatchlings are similar in appearance to the larvae of other mole salamanders, although, as with the marbleds, heavy mottling gives them a somewhat darker appearance. They transform into young terrestrial, and fossorial (burrowing), salamanders by late summer/early autumn. Their winters are spent underground in burrows not of their making.

One interesting behavior I've noticed in this salamander is that it will lift its tail when threatened. This behavior is an attempt to draw a predator to that part of the body, the loss of which is not vital to the salamander's survival because it grows back. After one taste of the tail, which exudes toxins, the predator should move on.

The tail is flattened on the dorsal sides, making this salamander a very good swimmer. This would be an advantage for an amphibian that utilizes larger bodies of water. The blue-spotteds' mottled pattern and coloration make them very difficult to spot when submerged.

As mentioned in the previous section, over the many years, the blue-spotted salamander has hybridized with the Jefferson salamander, forming a confusing complex of combinations. It often takes an expert, and/or DNA samples, to tell what percentage of each species makes up these hybrids. If the vent is surrounded by black, it is most likely *laterale*; if the vent is surrounded by gray, it is most likely jeffersonianum. Compared with *Jeffersons*, the overall ground color also tends to be darker in blue-spotteds.

This salamander has the distinction of being our northernmost

Ambystoma. Its range extends all the way up into the Hudson Bay area in the west and Labrador in the east. It is listed as Threatened in the state of Connecticut and of Special Concern in Vermont and Massachusetts. The hybrids are listed of Special Concern in Connecticut. While blue-spotteds come close to the border of Rhode Island, they are not known to occur in that state.

Hellbenders and Giant Salamanders
(Cryptobranchidae)

There are only three species of Cryptobranchidae, with one of them occurring in North America.

Eastern Hellbender
(*Cryptobranchus alleganiensis*)

They don't come much bigger than this one. With a size ranging between one foot and twenty-nine inches, adult Eastern hellbenders, North America's largest amphibian, have little to fear in the fast-flowing streams they inhabit. In addition to their size, they are protected by a poisonous mucusy secretion, earning them the nickname "snot otter" in some parts of their range. These salamanders are fully aquatic, but unlike mudpuppies, they lose their gills as they mature. Most of their oxygen is taken in through the skin, which is covered with long folds that increase the surface area for absorbtion. They will also come to the surface for an occasional gulp of air.

Hellbender nights are spent hunting (or ambushing) food among the rocks on the stream bed. Crayfish and small fish make up most of their diet, but they'll also eat frogs, worms, mollusks, and insects. They rest during the day beneath flat rocks in the water.

Breeding habits more closely resemble those of fish than of amphibians. Females lay their stringlike egg clusters in a saucer-shaped depression created by the male. The male then fertilizes them and stands guard. If he didn't, the eggs would be eaten by other hellbenders, including the females that lay the eggs.

Hellbenders can live for more than thirty years in the wild. The northern limit of their range falls within the Susquehanna and Allegheny River drainages in southern New York, where they are listed as a species of Special Concern.

Lungless, or Woodland, Salamanders
(Plethodontidae)

This is the largest group of salamanders, comprising 250 species, six of them found in New England, with four additional species in New York. *Plethodontidae* refers to the plethora of teeth within the mouths of the salamanders in this group. (Their teeth are actually parasphenoid teeth, projections found on the roof of the mouth.) Being lungless, these salamanders achieve gas exchange through their thin layer of skin and the lining of the mouth. All species sport a nasolabial groove—a narrow slit lined with glands, that runs from the nostrils to the upper lip. One of the functions of this feature is to drain water and dirt from the nostrils. The salamanders are also flanked on both sides by a series of vertical creases known as costal grooves.

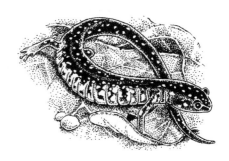

Slimy salamander,
Plethodon glutinosus

While most species in this family are terrestrial, half of the Northeast's Plethodons spend most of their time in or near water. They are known for elaborate courtship displays where the male will do anything in his power—head-butt, poke, push, prod, and rub—to get the female interested in picking up his spermatophore. Most of the females in this group brood their eggs to protect them from predation and desiccation.

Northern Dusky Salamander
(*Desmognathus fuscus*)

Dusky salamanders can be found in shallow streams, vernal pools, and seeps, sometimes side by side with two-lined salamanders. Duskys have a stocky look to them, with heavier legs than the two-lined, and are typically of a darker, more uniform color, especially in older individuals. Living up to their name, they grow duskier as they age, the darker pigment obscuring their patterns. However, their color is highly variable and ranges from dirty orange to dark gray/brown. Fine blue/gray speckling can often be seen along their sides. Their tails are flattened, with a dorsal keel, making them excellent swimmers.

I've noticed that when held in the hand, duskys wriggle in an eel-like motion and make little use of their legs. So, when handling, hold them close to the ground or water so they won't get injured if they slip away.

Duskys lay their eggs near, but out of, the water from midsummer into early autumn. The grapelike clusters of between ten and thirty eggs are deposited under logs, rocks, or within nooks and crannies of the streambed. The female stays with them, providing moisture and protection until they hatch. The larvae remain on land for a short period before entering the water to finish their development. The young are similar to two-lined larvae, but are larger, stockier, and have pairs of yellow spots bordered by a wavy dark band running down the back. They develop more rapidly, too, leaving the water within a year.

Dusky salamanders are common and widespread throughout the East.

Allegheny Mountain Dusky Salamander
(*Desmognathus ochrophaeus*)

New York State is host to another Desmognathus called the Allegheny mountain dusky salamander. This is one of six closely related species referred to collectively as the Ochrophaeus complex, but is the only one whose range extends into our region. (It can also be found as far north as southern Quebec and as far south as Tennessee.) This salamander is found at higher elevations than the other duskys—anywhere between six hundred and sixty-five hundred feet. Populations at the lower elevations tend to prefer seepage areas and springs. As they move up in altitude, their habitat preference changes to the cool, moist understory of conifer forests.

Allegheny mountain dusky salamanders can appear similar to Northern dusky salamanders, but *D. ochrophaeus* possesses a rounded tail, as opposed to the keeled tail of *D. fuscus*. Alleghenys vary in color from brown, olive, and gray to yellow or orange. All individuals have a pale stripe running from their eye to their jaw. Most have a broad strip down the back to the tail patterned with chevron-like markings. As individuals get older, their pattern fades and they appear overall dark brown.

Mating occurs between spring and fall. The female hangs a grapelike cluster of a dozen or two eggs under a rotting log or a flat stone, or deposits it in moss that is near, but not in, a stream. She stays with the eggs, standing guard until they hatch. (Alleghenys have, however, been known to eat that which they guard.) The newly eclosed larvae wriggle down to the water, where they remain for three weeks to eight months.

Alleghenys feed on a variety of terrestrial invertebrates—flies, worms, caterpillars, and snails. They are also fed upon by a number of birds and snakes. Like many plethodons, they can sacrifice their tail to a predator. The tail of this dusky is slightly longer than the body. If you come across an individual whose tail is shorter than the body, it could be that you're seeing the regrown tail, evidence of a successful escape.

Desmognathus ochrophaeus spend the winter in large congregations in seepage areas or heads of streams. They are widespread at higher elevations throughout New York. Because only one individual has been found in Vermont, they are listed as "hypothetical" in that state.

Northern Redback Salamander
(*Plethodon cinereus*)

The redback is our most common salamander. It's a small amphibian, ranging in length from two-and-a-half to four inches. A broad brick-red stripe runs down its back, tapering about halfway down the tail. Its sides are dark and often flecked with blue. It is a terrestrial species and can be found a good distance from water in deciduous and coniferous woodlands. A study conducted years ago concluded that the weight of all of the combined redbacks in a given area was more than all of the combined birds and about the same as all of the combined small mammals.

These salamanders are active year-round. I have found them under rocks, logs, and leaf litter during most months, including December. In fact, their courtship period can run from October to April. In the early summer, they lay their eggs inside rotten logs or beneath rocks. About a dozen or so are laid in a grapelike cluster, sometimes suspended from the roof of a small cavity, sometimes on the floor. The female stays with the eggs while they are developing. The larvae mature within those eggs, eliminating the need for water, and hatch as miniature versions of the adults about two months later.

The redbacks, like most salamanders, are primarily active at night, when they hunt for invertebrates in the leaf litter. This particular species will even do a little climbing into the bushes in search of a meal. They are most active on rainy nights, and can be found among the migrating salamander gang in the late winter rains.

Winters are spent in tunnels and burrows deep under the ground. On warm winter nights and days, redbacks do a little vertical migration to the surface, but the next cold snap sends them back down into the ground. They will also ride out the dry seasons underground, following root systems and crevices into the cooler, damper earth. While they do not require aquatic habitats for breeding, they still need to keep their skin moist.

There is a gray morph of the redback, and these specimens are referred to as lead-back salamanders. This form lacks the red stripe and the overall color ranges from light gray to nearly black to chestnut brown. I usually come across populations of either one morph or the other, but on occasion I've found mixed populations. In fact, I have both redbacks and lead-backs in my backyard. One way to tell that a salamander is a redback is to flip it over and have a look at the venter, or belly. In both forms, it is mottled with black and white.

There is also a rare orange form known as the erythristic redback salamander. There is some speculation that this form mimics the unpalatable red eft that shares its habitat.

Redbacks are common throughout the Northeast.

Northern Slimy Salamander
(*Plethodon glutinosus*)

Although it is found throughout southern New York, the Northern slimy salamander makes it into New England by the skin of its parasphenoid teeth. Its northeastern range reaches only the extreme western border of Connecticut and one area along the southern New Hampshire border. At least thirteen species of *Plethodon glutinosus* form a large complex that ranges across the country from the Midwest and then radiates southeast to Florida and northeast to our Connecticut and New Hampshire populations. The *northern* slimy salamander is the only one found here in the northeast, so it keeps things simple for us.

Slimys are black and shiny and riddled with large white spots along the flanks, with smaller, less concentrated spots along the back, head, and tail. They prefer mature second-growth forests where much of their time is spent below the leaf litter and under logs. As with most of the Caudata, they do come to the surface to search for food after a good rain and are primarily active between dawn and dusk.

Courtship and mating take place in the spring and autumn. In the late spring/early summer, the female lays a clutch of about half a dozen to three dozen eggs inside a decaying log and guards them until they hatch in the late summer. As with the redback salamander, metamorphosis occurs within the egg, so there is no aquatic stage. They can take between three to five years to mature, giving them plenty of time to attain their substantial size of eight inches. Winters are spent in the underground burrows made by small animals or in deep crevices within rock outcroppings. They will also go underground to ride out dry periods.

When handled, slimys exude a mucusy secretion, hence their name, although the secretion really feels more sticky than slimy. *Glutinosus* in Latin means "filled with glue." (I can attest from firsthand experience that this secretion is difficult to wash off.)

The northern slimy salamander is listed as Threatened in Connecticut.

•

A third amphibian bearing the Plethodon genus name, **Wehrle's salamander** (*Plethodon wehrlei*), occurs in the hills along the southwest border of New York and down into North Carolina. It is similar in size to the Northern Slimy, with the sides of its dark body covered with large, blotchy, pale spots, and the upper section (dorsum) flecked with many small, white spots.

Four-toed Salamander
(*Hemidactylium scutatum*)

The four-toed salamander is an alert-looking little amphibian that is active from late winter to late fall. As its name suggests, the number of toes (four, on the hind feet), distinguishes it from other salamanders, which have five toes on their hind feet. If you have a look at its underside, you will see an ivory white belly peppered with heavy black spots. This will help distinguish it from any other woodland salamander you may encounter.

The tail of this species has a notable constriction at the base and is detachable. If a predator—or heavy-handed human admirer—grabs the salamander, the tail snaps off and twitches. It continues to move on its own, distracting the predator from the more vulnerable parts, namely the salamander itself. The tail will soon be regenerated.

The terrestrial four-toeds can be found in deciduous forests under rocks and logs. However, they are usually in close proximity to wet, boggy areas.

In New England, mating takes place in the late summer and early autumn. Come the following late winter/early spring rains, they migrate from their subterranean wintering quarters to lay eggs. They are often found traveling alongside the other early season amphibians stirred by the early rains.

Four-toeds prefer to deposit their eggs in clumps of sphagnum moss along the edges of water. About three or four dozen eggs are laid singly and, as with many in the Plethodon family, are guarded by the female throughout their development. Upon hatching, the larvae wriggle through the moss and drop into the water. They leave the water in about a month and a half.

Scutatum is found in all of the New England states and New York; however, its distribution is spotty at best. One of the reasons for this spottiness is its preference of habitat—areas of wet sphagnum moss surrounded by woodlands. This isn't always easy to come by. It is listed as a species of Special Concern in Massachusetts and Vermont. In Maine, it is found in only a couple of regions in the extreme south and central east.

Northern Spring Salamander
(*Gyrinophilus p. porphyriticus*)

Spring salamanders are the second largest salamander species in the Northeast, some attaining a length of eight and a half inches. Their name comes from their habitat, not their preference of season, as they are active year-round.

These sturdy, dirty-orange salamanders are primarily creatures of stream edges. They can be spotted, with luck, by flipping over flat, partially submerged rocks. They are generally found in cool, pristine, moving water, but will also inhabit shady seeps and will even go walkabout in upland areas when it's raining. Moving water provides high oxygen content, a big plus for these large skin-breathing Caudata.

This is an animal perfectly suited for its habitat, too. Its heavy body is flattened, making it possible for it to hug the bottom along the edges of a fast flowing stream. The keeled tail thins out at the tip, allowing it to move rapidly underwater. It feeds on a variety of animals smaller than itself, mostly insects, and has been known to eat other salamanders such as duskys and two-lined salamanders. It is also not above eating the occasional young spring salamander.

The eggs are laid in the early summer and are attached singly to the underside of a flat submerged rock. The mother guards them until they hatch in the late summer/early fall. The larvae can take up to four years to develop. In fact, the genus name of *Gyrinophilus* comes from the Greek word *gyrinos*, meaning tadpole and *phil* or *philos*, meaning loving. In other words, the spring salamander loves being a tadpole so much it remains one for years.

Overwintering takes place in a burrow in the wet soil by a stream or river. They can remain active within those burrows throughout the cold season.

While found throughout the Northeast, the Northern spring salamander is listed as Threatened in Connecticut, and of Special Concern in Massachusetts. It is very rare in Rhode Island, but common in Vermont and New Hampshire. Its northernmost New England range extends into southwest Maine.

Northern Red Salamander
(*Pseudotriton ruber ruber*)

Northern red salamanders are found in scattered sites in southernmost New York state. They are part of a complex of four similar species, with *P. ruber ruber* making it farthest north.

Red salamanders are chunky creatures, and colorful, too—salmon pink to bright red, covered with many black dots.

Northern Two-Lined Salamander
(*Eurycea bislineata*)

Flip over a flat rock in a shallow stream and you may be rewarded with the find of a two-lined salamander. These amphibians spend most of their active life in or near brooks, where they hunt for insects and tiny crustaceans. They can also be found along the edges of vernal pools and in a variety of other habitats, and will also wander into the forest to take up residence under rotting logs. Breeding season runs between autumn and spring. Their eggs are laid underwater, where they are attached to plants or beneath submerged rocks and logs. The adult females stay nearby to keep an eye on things. They can take aggressive action, such as posturing, snapping, or biting, to repel intruders.

The adults somewhat resemble the abundant redback salamander. However, the two black-bordered yellowish stripes that run down the two-lined salamander's dorsal sides are lacking in the redbacks. The two-lined has a more slender look, too, with a long, thin tail that exceeds the length of its body.

Two-lined salamanders have a very long season of activity. I've found adults from February to November, and I've also come across their larvae at different times of the year. The young can take a few years to develop and can grow to a good size. They are pinkish-orange and speckled with darker markings on most of the body. This speckling can often give them a dusky look. Like all salamander larvae, they have tendrilly gills behind the head and are active hunters. They feed upon isopods, amphipods, and other little creatures on the streambed.

One particular behavior I've noticed in the adults is that they will flip themselves into the air when disturbed. This is most likely a startle and/or escape defense.

Bislineata are common and widespread throughout the northeastern states.

•

The **long-tailed salamander** (*Eurycea l. longicauda*) is another Eurycea species that just makes it into the Northeast. It is found from southern New York down to northern Alabama. It is among the larger Eurycea, with a tail that can account for up to 65 percent of its body length. Long-tailed salamanders are an attractive species—golden brown and covered with irregular rows of heavy black spots.

NEWTS
(Salamandridae)

Six species of newts live in North America, but only one of them, the Eastern newt, occurs in the Northeast. Eastern newts are broken down into four subspecies, and ours is the red-spotted newt.

Unlike their slimy-skinned salamander relatives, newts have rough-textured, drier skin. Their costal grooves are also indistinct.

Red-spotted Newt
(*Notophthalmus viridescens*)

Next time you are near a beaver pond, pause to search for the salamander with three lives. The mature red-spotted newt is an aquatic creature, spending most of its time in ponds, small lakes, and quiet areas in a variety of watercourses. (I rarely come across a beaver pond without one in it.) The adult newt ranges in color from olive-green to dark brown. Its body is peppered with small black spots, and larger black-bordered spots run down its side. The tail is keeled, almost finlike, which aids it in swimming. While this is an aquatic animal, it is still air-breathing, although it most likely supplements its oxygen intake through its skin.

Breeding usually takes place from spring to late summer. The male approaches the female and rubs his chin, which contains glands that produce a stimulant, on the female's head. Should she decide to accept his offer of spermatophores, she picks them up in her cloaca and proceeds to lay eggs within a short time. The eggs are laid singly, up to about four

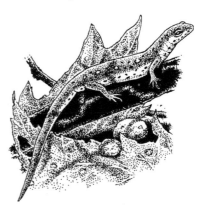

Red-spotted newt, Notophtalmus viridescens (*adult*)

hundred of them, on the stems of submerged vegetation. They hatch in a month or so.

The larvae are similar to other aquatic salamander larvae. They are a pale yellow-green and have large, feathery gills. Unlike the adults, which are active during the day, the larvae are primarily nocturnal as they hunt for tiny crustaceans, insect larvae, and mollusks. During the course of about three months, the larvae will develop lungs to replace those gills, and their skin will grow rough and bright orange. It is now time for the next stage, the red eft.

While efts can still be found in the water, this stage allows them to travel across the land and colonize new ponds. Their bright color warns predators of their toxicity. Since they are inedible to most animals, the efts have little problem traversing the forest floor during the daylight hours.

After between two and six years on land, the red-spotted newt begins to transform once again. This time, it changes from its terrestrial form back to a creature better suited for living underwater. It changes color to blend with the brown/green of a pond's bottom, and the tail flattens out into a caudal fin. It re-enters the aquatic world to live out the rest of its years as an air-breathing, yet aquatic, salamander.

Most newts, adults and efts, spend the winter beneath logs and leaf litter. Some adults colonize permanent bodies of water and can stay there year-round.

The red-spotted newt is found throughout the Northeast.

MUDPUPPIES
(Proteidae)

There are five species of Proteidae in North America. The name refers to Proteus, a Greek sea god who took many forms. I think that name would be better suited to any group of amphibians *but* the Proteidae, as this is the one group that really *doesn't* change its form.

In our area, we get the species that is commonly called the mudpuppy (*Necturus maculosus*), or occasionally the waterdog, although that name is most often reserved for species other than *N. maculosus*. It was believed by some that these amphibians would bark when disturbed, hence the name.

(They don't, though.) What all Proteidae have in common is that they are, in essence, permanent aquatic larvae with gills, and they all have four toes on each foot.

Mudpuppy, Necturus maculosus

Northern Mudpuppy
(*Necturus maculosus*)

With records of lengths of nearly twenty inches, mudpuppies give the other largest American salamanders, the hellbenders, a run for their money. Adult mudpuppies are more typically between eight and fourteen inches, but even at the smaller end of the scale, their size leaves little question as to their identity.

Mudpuppies took a different route on the evolutionary trail—or perhaps it would be more accurate to say that they stayed the course while all the other salamanders veered off the path. Unlike most of the Caudata we encounter in the Northeast, mudpuppies never leave the water. They are considered neotonic, meaning that, aside from their ability to reproduce, they retain their larval traits.

They have a primordial look to them, perhaps resembling one of those first aquatic creatures poised to gain purchase on the land. They've kept their gills, and the gills are long and bushy, an adaptation suited for the muddy waters they inhabit. (Larger gills allow more surface area for absorbing oxygen. In other salamanders that have gills during a stage of their life, the appendages are smaller, as the water they inhabit is usually cooler and clearer, and therefore, more oxygenated.) In addition to gills, mudpuppies also have a pair of lungs. The lungs serve a supplemental purpose and undoubtedly aid in keeping the salamander alive during strandings and/or times of high water viscosity. They are also most likely used for the purpose most lungs evolved *from*—swim bladders. These organs, found in most fish, allow the animal to control its buoyancy in the water.

Mudpuppies mate in autumn, and the females lay their eggs in the following spring. The eggs, between thirty and two hundred, are attached singly to the underside of submerged logs and rocks, and the mother usually lingers in the vicinity to offer protection. The inch-long larvae hatch six to eight weeks later. Unlike most salamander larvae, those of the mudpuppies are equipped with front legs and toes at the onset of their development. Their hind legs are also present, but look like little bumps. They will eventually have four toes on each foot. Two wide yellow stripes run along their dorsolateral edges, but the stripes disappear as the mudpuppies mature. It takes them between four and six years to reach sexual maturity, and they generally add an inch or so of growth each year.

Adult mudpuppies are gray brown. The mottling of pale yellow spots in the juveniles becomes deep blue in the adults. That rather dull, cryptic coloration is offset by the pair of large, feathery maroon gills that wave in the current like tendrils of little sea anemones. Since mudpuppies are fully aquatic, their tail is dorsally flattened to give better propulsion along a river or streambed. The tail may also be used to supplement oxygen absorption.

Mudpuppies are generally nocturnal. They are active predators and eat insects, fish, snails, frogs, leeches, other salamanders, crayfish, and a wide variety of other aquatic organisms, including plants. They are probably encountered more by fishermen than by herpetologists, as they are not above snatching a meal from the end of a fishing line. They are found in lakes, rivers, and canals throughout the seasons in all of the northeastern states; however, it is believed that they are an introduced species in many of the sites in New England. One exception is Lake Champlain, in Vermont, where their status is currently listed as Special Concern.

SPADEFOOT TOADS
(Pelobatidae)

This group of amphibians is linked by a number of characteristics, the most obvious being the single sharp horn, or tubercle, on the inner surface of each hind foot. This would be the spade the frog is named for and it is indeed used for digging into the sand. (True toads also bear tubercles, but they are not as pronounced as in the spadefoot.) The Pelobatidae also have catlike vertically elliptical pupils, which set them apart from the rest of the frogs, which have horizontal pupils. The skin of a spadefoot is smooth, with small, scattered warts. They lack the large parotoid glands of true toads, but can exude a strong toxin through their skin.

An Eastern spadefoot toad,
Scaphiopus holbrookii holbrookii,
burying itself in the sand

Spadefoots have evolved to take advantage of arid environments. During dry periods a spadefoot will burrow into the sand and wait it out within a protective chamber created by its skin fluid. They are explosive breeders, emerging during torrential downpours to gather in the newly created ponds. Amplexus is achieved when the male grabs the female around the waist. This is unique in frogs, where the male usually grabs the female under the arms. While they will also breed in more permanent bodies of water, spadefoots often breed in temporary pools, and their tadpoles are prepared to get out of there fast, developing into toadlets in as little as two weeks.

There are five species of spadefoot toads in North America. We have one of them in the Northeast.

Eastern Spadefoot
(*Scaphiopus holbrookii*)

The scientific name for this genus comes from the Greek *skaphis*, which means shovel or spade, and *pous*, meaning foot. The species name honors John Edward Holbrook, a nineteenth-century herpetologist, whom some have dubbed the father of North American herpetology.

Our spadefoot is a stout little creature, brown to olive in color with two irregular creamy lines running down its back. Eyes, feet, etc., are as described in the family account above.

On any night between April and September, low barometric pressure and heavy rains draw these toads from their burrows to where they converge around pools and ponds. They dwell in areas with loose, loamy soils or sand, which allows them to dig. The males call in the females with their loud, nasal, crowlike caws. (The call may even be indelicately described as a short fart.) The individual call is brief, but when added to the surrounding chorus creates a sustained noise (although music to *my* ears) that gives a backyard herpetologist his or her best shot at finding one.

Eggs are laid in short, gelatinous bands attached to or among the aquatic plants. The tadpoles emerge days later. They feed on algae and plankton and are not above a little scavenging. They leave the water somewhere between two weeks and two months later, depending on the condition of their habitat and the population density. Neither juveniles nor adults travel far from their natal habitats. They're most active at night, which, along with their penchant for tunneling, makes them very difficult to locate. Your best chance to find one is to go out on one of those miserable rainy nights, check the roads bisecting the appropriate habitats, and listen for the calls. The adults disperse from the breeding pools within a couple days after breeding, creating a very small window of opportunity for finding them.

Spadefoots overwinter in underground burrows and are inactive until the following spring. They are found in New York (mostly on Long Island), Connecticut, where they are listed as Endangered, and in Massachusetts (particularly on Cape Cod) and Rhode Island, where they are listed as Threatened.

TRUE TOADS
(Bufonidae)

Toads are frogs. Frogs, on the other hand, are not necessarily toads. Several characteristics that make a toad a toad are obvious to the casual observer. For one, their skin is dry and bumpy, whereas the skin of many

An American toad, Bufo americanus, *in a "toad house"*

other frogs, such as the true frogs, is smooth and somewhat slippery. Toads tend to lean toward a boxy, squat appearance. If toads were dogs, they'd be bulldogs. Most have a pair of enlarged poison-generating organs called parotoid (meaning next to ear) glands on the top of the head. A predator that picks up one of these amphibians in its mouth will get an unpleasant surprise. The poison causes immediate irritation of the mouth tissues, and if enough is ingested it can lead to vomiting, cardiac irregularities, and sometimes, death. Toads can also puff up their bodies, a defense possibly designed to foil being swallowed by snakes, which are unaffected by the parotoid gland toxins.

Another characteristic that makes a toad a toad is the lack of teeth, which are present in the upper jaw of most frogs.

Most toads move in short hops or just crawl, unlike other frogs, which tend to leap. While water is necessary for breeding and egg laying, toads can also be found pretty far from water. Their eggs are laid in long strands, very often in temporary bodies of water. As a result, they've evolved to develop very quickly. Incidentally, a group of toads is called a knot. (I think this would better apply to a group of egg strands.)

We have eighteen species of true toads in North America, two of them occurring in the Northeast.

AMERICAN TOAD
(*Bufo americanus*)

For such a rough-looking creature, the American toad has been blessed with the sweetest call of all the frogs. Its melodious trill is a soothing sound that emanates from the spring forest.

Toads may not be pretty, but a case could be made for their appearance to be described as compelling. They are stocky, brown to gray (sometimes brick red), with paler colors creating a jumbled pattern above, on the arms and legs. Their bellies are white and heavily mottled with black spots from their chins to their chests. Males have black throats. Dark blotches

A garter snake swallowing an American toad

on the dorsum (upper area) and arms and legs contain one or two large warts, often red or pale brown. The number of warts, one or two, helps distinguish this toad from the similar-looking Fowler's toad, which has three or more warts within each blotch. So, too, do the parotoid glands, which in the American toad are kidney shaped and disconnected from, or barely touching, the ridge right behind the eye. In Fowler's toads, the glands tend to be thinner and are pressed right up against those ridges. You can also have a look at the venter, or belly. As described above, in the American toad, it's heavily mottled with black. Fowler's venter is clean, with a small dark spot on the chest.

American toads begin their mating call shortly after their mid-March emergence. They gather along the edges of a variety of aquatic habitats in April to mate. Their long strands of eggs snake and intertwine among the vegetation along the basin. It is not unusual to come across these strands in water-filled tire ruts. The eggs develop very rapidly, as do the tadpoles. The tadpoles are inky black, with clear tail fins that are slightly rounded at the end.

When they leave the water as toadlets, they embark on a terrestrial life in deciduous forests, fields, and gardens, where they help keep down the slug population. Some people make little toad shelters in their vegetable gardens in order to entice these predators of garden pests. These are simple structures that are made by placing a flat rock (roof) across two stones (walls). The toads are mostly active at night and rest in shaded shelters to escape the hot sun. In the fall, they seek an underground burrow to wait out the cold weather.

American toads have fairly long life spans. In the wild, they can live up to a decade and have been known to triple that number in captivity. They are common and widespread throughout the Northeast.

Fowler's Toad
(Bufo woodhousii fowleri)

Fowler's toads were once considered a subspecies of the Woodhouse toad. They are now recognized as a species in and of themselves. They are named for Samuel P. Fowler, who founded the Natural History Department at the Essex Institute in Salem, Massachusetts, and who discovered this frog in 1843.

The early naturalist's namesakes sleep just a little later than the American toads, emerging in late April/early May. Their call sounds like that of an angry sheep, a nasal *waaaaaaaaahhhh* that lasts for a few seconds. They have a tidier look to them when compared with *americanus*. Perhaps it has something to do with their smoother skin. Their patterns are more distinct, too, with the markings more in contrast with a paler and grayer body. But beware: Fowler's and *americanus* can hybridize, making identification more difficult. This is more likely to happen where the two habitats overlap in the deciduous forest. In this situation, a toad in the sand is most likely a Fowler's. A toad in the woods could be either. For differences between the species, see the description of American toads above.

As mentioned, Fowler's generally prefer a different habitat from their *americanus* cousins, and they populate sandy, dry, and well-drained areas. They also lay their eggs in long strands, often in temporary bodies of water. I once found a large population of tadpoles in the corner of a flooded parking lot along a beach in Madison, Connecticut. They had metamorphosed into toadlets and dispersed by the time the water evaporated. Like those of the Americans, the Fowler's tadpoles are deep black. Closer inspection reveals tiny flecks of red and white.

Fowler's toads are mostly active at night, but I've seen them out and about during the day. They tend to turn in a few weeks earlier than their other Bufonidae cousins, entering their underground burrows around September. They are found irregularly throughout all of the northeastern states, with the exception of Maine (if they are there, they're hiding out at the very southern tip), and are listed as being of Special Concern in Vermont, where they are found in the eastern portion of the state.

TREEFROGS, CRICKET FROGS, AND CHORUS FROGS
(Hylidae)

The Hylidae are typically lean and small, with sticky toe pads that allow them to cling to vertical surfaces. Extra cartilage between the last two bones of each toe enables the tip of the toe to pivot, swivel, and lay flat against all surfaces.

The males are often incessant callers, setting up their territories around the perimeter of a body of water. Many call from the surrounding vegetation and move down into the water, often riding on the back of the female, to mate.

Hylidae is one of the largest families of Anurans, with twenty-six species in North America and four in the Northeast.

The **Northern Cricket Frog** (*Acris c. crepitans*) is the Northeast's only representative of the cricket frogs. Its northern range barely makes it into southern portion of New York, where it is listed as an Endangered species.

Gray Treefrog
(*Hyla versicolor*)

Gray treefrogs are arboreal frogs with bumpy skin that ranges in color from ashy gray to dark gray. The base color changes with temperature, as their scientific name, *versicolor*, suggests. (*Hyla* means "of the woods.") The cooler it gets, the darker the frogs become. As they warm, their base color pales considerably and is often covered with large, lichen-green patterns. This coloration helps them blend very well with the lichen-covered trees they inhabit. *Versicolor* is at the larger end of the scale when it comes to treefrogs, and it has ample-sized toe pads. It is not unusual to find one clinging to the glass of a storm door or window as it hunts for insects attracted to the light. I've found this group to be very tame when handled.

These frogs emerge from their wintering burrows around April. They move to trees surrounding their breeding pools in May and begin to call. The call is a loud, quivering trill that can go day and night during the peak of the breeding season. Because many males may surround a pool, which can act as an amplifier, their chorus can be heard from quite a distance. At first, it would take me a moment to distinguish between the call of a red-bellied woodpecker and that of a treefrog. Eventually, I figured out that if it is moving from tree to tree, it's a woodpecker, and if it is stationary, it's a gray treefrog. The call also sounds a bit like a young raccoon, further complicating the issue.

The females approach the calling males, who grab on and ride them down to the water where the egg laying and fertilization takes place. The breeding period for this species can last more than two months.

The eggs, up to two thousand per female, are laid in floating mats in groups of a dozen to three dozen. Gray treefrogs utilize a variety of standing-water habitats, including swimming pool covers. Their preferred habitats are red maple swamps and shrubby wetlands, but again, they're quite cosmopolitan. The eggs hatch less than a week later. Of all of the tadpoles, I find theirs the easiest to recognize, as their tails are brick red, possibly suggesting unpalatability to would-be predators. They are also among the last to be found in the water as summer comes to an end. (This is barring, of course, the tadpoles of green frogs and bullfrogs, which can overwinter in this stage.) The tadpoles are filter feeders, trapping suspended particles of phytoplankton and other detritus.

The gray treefroglets appear in late summer and look nothing like the adults. They could be mistaken for spring peepers as they cling to the leaves in low vegetation. However, they are green, not ochre, are relatively unmarked, and have boxier heads than the pointy-headed peepers. They also share with the adults a tendency to rest with their arms tucked under their chest, offering up some amusing anthropomorphic observa-

Gray Treefrog, Hyla versicolor

tions. (In reality, this posture could play a role in decreasing their profile.)

Gray treefrogs overwinter beneath the leaf litter and can withstand freezing temperatures. Blood alcohol transferred to the vital organs protects the cells in those organs from bursting when the frogs thaw.

Hyla versicolor is found in all of the northeastern states.

Spring Peeper
(*Pseudacris crucifer*)

The spring peeper is our smallest frog, and one of the first to begin chorusing. The genus Pseudacris puts it in the group known as chorus frogs. It is a "false *acris*." (Acris is the genus of the cricket frogs, which, like the peepers, have a pointed head, but unlike the peepers, do not climb.) Peepers have a base color of ochre with a large brown cross on their backs, hence the species name of *crucifer*. They were once considered to be in the genus *Hyla*, but their smaller toe pads and preference for perching in lower vegetation, rather than trees, knocked them out of that family about a decade ago.

Peepers peep—or, as some describe it, *preep*. Their peeping can be heard from great distances and can be almost deafening if you are standing in the middle of a chorusing congregation. This takes place throughout the seasons, but is most prevalent during their breeding period between late March and May, which is also the best time to seek them out. The males climb onto the low vegetation, rarely higher than three feet, growing around the edges of a variety of wetland habitats—vernal pools, ponds, swamps, pretty much anything that holds water. Then they begin to peep and peep and peep. While the peak chorusing takes place at night, they call, with less tenacity, during the day as well. The calls, which vary in intent and therefore in sound, serve to attract females, establish territory, and ward off competition. The females, which are silent, select their mates by swimming nearby and making contact. The male climbs aboard, and fertilization takes place beneath the surface of the water.

The female lays her eggs singly, and either attaches them to aquatic vegetation or beneath the leaf litter at the bottom of the pond. Up to nine hundred can be laid by a single individual. The eggs hatch in about a week, and the tadpoles feed on algae and detritus.

The newly metamorphosed froglets leave the water about two months later. They linger around their breeding pool, reclaiming nutrients as they absorb their tail. Then they disperse to the surrounding area. Peeper habitats vary greatly, but they are most often found in damp deciduous (sometimes coniferous) woods, meadows, and fields, where they feed on a variety of invertebrates. They are most active at night, but rainy and humid days get them moving as well.

Peepers overwinter above the frost line beneath the leaf litter. As with gray treefrogs and wood frogs, they can withstand freezing temperatures. The ability to pump sugar-rich blood into vital organs, such as the heart and lungs, keeps those organs from freezing. The rest of the body can freeze without detrimental effects. This capacity to withstand cold conditions gives peepers a jump on the breeding season.

Although they are in a state of hibernation at this point, peepers can still be awakened on a warm winter afternoon, sometimes to the point where they are actually compelled to vocalize. I have heard spring peepers peeping in every month of the year in Connecticut. Hearing that harbinger of spring on a sunny, snow-covered February afternoon is most heartening. These tantalizing February trills are short-lived, though, usually with only a few notes.

Spring peepers are common in all of the northeastern states.

Western Chorus Frog
(*Pseudacris triseriata*)

Western, or striped, chorus frogs are another "false *acris*" found in the Northeast region. They are small, like peepers, smooth-skinned, and range in color from brown to greenish-gray. The species name of *triseriata*, meaning "three stripes," calls attention to the three dark stripes running down the frog's back. The stripes can be either solid or broken, so a more consistent distinguishing characteristic is a white line along the upper lip.

Western chorus frogs are found in a wide variety of habitats, but tend to stick close to woodlands. Originally a prairie species, they have expanded their range and habitat to adapt to the diminishing grasslands and can be quite cosmopolitan, being found in heavily populated, even urban, areas.

These frogs are very early risers and begin their breeding season in late winter/early spring. Their call is a short, rising trill, or a *prreeeep* that sounds very similar to a fingernail being run over the teeth of a comb. Eggs are laid in small clusters in vernal pools surrounded by dense shrubs. Having small toepads allows the frogs to climb these plants, but they don't make it very high.

After breeding and egg-laying, the chorus frogs leave the water and spend their active season in the surrounding fields and woods. The tadpoles develop quickly to prevent stranding in the shrinking pools. They linger around the edges for a while and then join the adults in the dryer areas.

As with the spring peeper and wood frog, western chorus frogs are freeze-tolerant. They spend the winter beneath rocks and logs near their breeding ponds.

Their eastern limit lies mostly along the northwestern borders of New York and Vermont (where they are listed as Endangered) and up into Canada.

TRUE FROGS
(Ranidae)

The true frogs, semiaquatic Anurans, are generally on the large end of the size scale when compared with frogs in other families. In fact, this family contains the goliath frog (*Conraua goliath*), an African giant that can measure three feet from head to toe and weigh up to seven pounds.

Much of a true frog's time is spent in the water, where it breeds, feeds, escapes terrestrial predators, and overwinters. It has webbed feet, horizontal pupils, a pointed snout, and long hind legs. The latter attribute contributes to its ability to leap, which is the frog's typical mode of travel when on land.

During breeding season, the thumbs and forearms of the males swell, allowing them to hold on tightly beneath the forearms of the females.

North America is home to twenty-one species of Ranidae, seven of them occurring in the Northeast.

Bullfrog
(*Rana catesbeiana*)

With a body length that can reach eight inches, the bullfrog is North America's largest frog. Their common name makes reference to their size—big as a bull. The species name, *catesbeiana*, honors Mark Catesby, an early eighteenth-century English naturalist who wrote the two-volume *Natural History of Carolina, Florida and the Bahama Islands.*

Bullfrogs are olive-brown above and covered with small bumps, or tubercles. Below, they are creamy white. Males have yellow throats. The tympanic membranes, or ears, are clearly evident behind the eyes and can also be used to sex the individuals. In males, the disk is one and a half times larger than the diameter of the eye. In females, it is about the same size as the eye.

Bullfrog, Rana catesbeiana

In bullfrogs, the supratympanic fold, or ridge, begins behind the eye and wraps around the tympanic membrane. In the similar-looking green frog, the fold, called the dorsolateral ridge, continues all the way down the dorsal sides of the frog, coming to an end just prior to reaching the rump. While it would be difficult to confuse a large adult bullfrog with a green frog, a younger, smaller bullfrog could present more of a challenge.

Bullfrogs are found in a variety of freshwater habitats that retain water year-round. These are the frogs that spend much of their time along the vegetated edges of the larger lakes and ponds. They have a long breeding period—between May and early August; however, the larger adult males are preceded to the breeding grounds by the younger frogs in April. The breeding begins with the call of the males, that deep, basso *jug-o-rum*. It is a sound that can be felt in the chest as well as heard. The males are highly territorial and will challenge all comers entering their area, unless it's a female. Attracted by some quality evident only to another bullfrog, the female enters the male's zone and makes physical contact, initiating him to grab onto her back. Fertilization takes place in the male's territory, and the female lays a floating mass of between ten and twenty thousand eggs among the vegetation along the edge. The eggs gradually sink below the surface, where they hatch between one and three weeks later.

The tadpoles feed on vegetation and detritus and can take up to three years to develop. The typical time period, however, is between one and two years. They are muddy green in color and will grow to the size of a small chicken egg before leaving the water. The newly transformed froglets band together in the shallows along the water's edge. One of their biggest threats comes in the form of other adult bullfrogs, which are not above eating their own kind.

The appetite of bullfrogs is legend, with stories of them eating snakes, birds, and other bullfrogs. It is generally accepted that, if it moves, the bullfrog will eat it. (There is a report that a bullfrog in southern Connecticut actually ate a small dachshund, though the story is suspect, because I'm the one who made it up. However, if a bullfrog *could* fit a small dog down its throat, I have no doubt it would try.)

Rana catesbeiana overwinter on the lake or pond bottom beneath the leaf litter and/or mud. There they remain in a state of semihibernation, all bodily functions drastically slowed and fed by oxygen extracted through the skin. The advantage of this is obvious in amphibians that cannot withstand freezing temperatures. While the water is plenty cold (and oxygenated), few permanent lakes and ponds freeze all the way down to the bottom. Should the frog choose to hibernate out of the water, it would have to find a burrow below the frost line, which could require it to go several feet down.

Bullfrogs are common in all of the northeastern states, and are becoming more common in southern states where they have been introduced. Many consider them a threat to native populations of smaller frogs.

Green Frog
(*Rana clamitans*)

The green frog is a frog's frog. It is the frog that comes to mind when one thinks of frogs. All that's missing is the stereotypical *ribit*. Green frogs don't *ribit* (the Pacific treefrog is the one that provides that call so often associated with frogs). Green frogs *pluck*. The sound is explosive and is often likened to the sound of a picked banjo string. In fact, the call of the green frog is what led the species to be named *clamitans*, which means loud, as in clamor. (I have found that you can get them to respond if you imitate their call.)

Green frogs are similar to bullfrogs in appearance. The major differences lie in the size (green frogs are smaller) and the dorsolateral ridge, which is absent in bullfrogs. They are olive-green and are often covered with dark splotches. In rare instances, they can be turquoise (which also occurs in bullfrog populations); some call these forms blue frogs. The males, as with bullfrogs, can be distinguished from the females by the yellow throat and a tympanic membrane that is larger in diameter than the eye. Green frogs frequent a variety of water bodies, from vernal pools to lakes, although their eggs are most often laid in permanent bodies of water, which is important because the tadpoles can take an extra year to develop.

Green frogs emerge from their winter quarters in late March/early April and are sometimes found among the migrating spotted salamanders on rainy nights. The young frogs, usually males, which left the water by the end of the previous summer, tend to appear prior to the adults. By early May, they are all in place along the water's edge, and we begin to hear their calls. Male green frogs are highly territorial and tend to remain in their chosen strongholds throughout the two-month breeding season. The female selects the male who seems to have chosen the most secure spot to lay her eggs. This takes place in the shallow, vegetated areas along the edge of the water. Up to four thousand eggs are laid in a sheet, and hatch in less than a week. Spreading the eggs in a shallow layer allows the sun to warm each egg at the same rate. Its effect is akin to floating a solar panel on the water's surface.

The tadpoles are olive above, with dark mottling and cream below.

They feed on algae and detritus. Ones hatched from eggs laid earlier in the season will develop that year; the later arrivals will overwinter as tadpoles and develop in the following spring or summer.

Like most true frogs, the greens overwinter on the pond floor. They are very dark at his stage, blending perfectly with the color of the pond floor. They are not as deep sleepers as many other species and have been known to stir throughout the season, though they probably don't feed much or at all. Because their bodily functions need to be slowed to conserve energy, the digestive system would be hard pressed to deal with a big meal.

Green frogs are common throughout all of the northeastern states.

Mink Frog
(*Rana septentrionalis*)

New England is considered the northern end of the range for most amphibians. The mink frogs, however, are primarily frogs of the north (*septentrionalis* means northern) with northern New York, Vermont, New Hampshire, and Maine being the *southern* end of their range.

They are very similar in appearance to green frogs, but tend to be smaller. They are muddy green above and covered with large, irregular dark spots. The patterns and coloring are variable, as are the dorsolateral ridges, which range from strongly present to missing entirely. Green frogs are consistently found with dorsolateral ridges and with dark bands on the legs, a feature absent in the minks. The most reliable way to tell them apart is to look at the hind feet. The webbing on the hind feet of the mink frog reaches the last joint of the longest toe, while the webbing of the green frog barely makes it to the second joint of the longest toe. You could also just give the frog a sniff. The mink reference comes from their musky odor; some describe it as oniony. This is meant to serve as a defense from predators; however, mink frogs *are* eaten by a number of animals, including raccoons and herons.

They inhabit cold waters with emergent vegetation and are often found in the shallow, vegetated areas during the day and on lily pads at night. Good places to look for them are where streams enter or exit from ponds and lakes, or in peaty bogs. Mink frogs can be very secretive, and when threatened will dive down into the mud or vegetation. Their call— *cut . . . cut . . . cut*—given from the water or from atop a lily pad, is similar to that of a green frog's, but is higher and slightly metallic. It has been likened to someone hammering a nail into a shingle.

The breeding period of mink frogs is later than that of most frogs and occurs between June and August. Eggs, between four hundred and a thousand per frog, are laid in a gelatinous mass attached to submerged vegetation. Some mink frog tadpoles may transform into froglets in late summer, but many overwinter and change the following summer.

Mink frogs are highly aquatic and rarely leave the water. They dry out very quickly. Only on rainy nights will they venture across the land. While found in New York, Vermont, New Hampshire, and Maine, they are uncommon in (or absent from) the southern portions of these states.

Pickerel Frog
(*Rana palustris*)

Palustris is Latin for "of the marsh," suggesting where these frogs can be found. Marshes are just one of many habitats pickerel frogs utilize, however. Unlike the three previous true frogs described above, these amphibians spend little time actually in the water, although a stream, lake, pond, or pool is usually in the vicinity. They like swamps, meadows, bogs, fens, and lawns, the latter making grass mowing a challenge.

The patterns on pickerel frogs are designed to help them blend in with the moist, vegetated habitats in which they dwell. They are medium-sized, fairly slender, with a bronze base color and two parallel rows of rectangular spots running down the dorsum. A cream-colored line runs along each of the dorsolateral ridges. The ventral area is white, except for the waist and legs, which are yellow-orange, giving the appearance of a pair of bright *lederhosen*. The common name probably also makes reference to the similar color found on the fish of the same name. This coloration is a warning to predators that this frog will not taste very good.

Pickerel frogs are early spring risers and can be found among the migrating throng of salamanders in mid- to late March. Their breeding season runs between April and mid-May, which is about the only time you will actually see them in the water. The male's call, often made from underwater, sounds like a quiet, lazy snore. It reminds me of the sound two balloons make when rubbed together. It sneaks up on you; you hear it before you realize you are hearing it.

The female chooses her mate, and he climbs aboard, sometimes clinging to her back for days and holding on even when his job of fertilizing her eggs is complete. They soon leave the breeding pools to return to the surrounding habitat.

An average of twenty-five hundred eggs are laid and are attached to the submerged vegetation. They are held together within a gelatinous mass similar in shape and appearance to those of the mole salamanders and wood frogs. However, unlike the solid-black embryos of those species, pickerel frog eggs are half brown and half pale yellow. There are also about three times as many within the mass. They hatch within two or three weeks. The tadpoles are greenish yellow with a pointy tail and clear fins, and they develop more rapidly than their other Ranidae cousins, becoming froglets before the end of the season. By the middle to end of summer, they've dispersed into the surrounding vegetation. The metamorphs look like miniature versions of the adults and are very active hunters. They, like the adults, are quick jumpers and always seem to have an escape route planned in advance.

As with most true frogs, the pickerel frog hibernates underwater. In the Northeast they are found in every state, where they are fairly common.

Northern Leopard Frog
(Rana pipiens)

People often mistake the pickerel frog for the leopard frog. Perhaps the spots that mark both species are more easily identified with a leopard than with a fish. Leopard frogs are also the ones used for dissection in high school biology, which could add to the familiarity of the name. Like *Rana palustris*, they are frogs of the grass, are covered with large brown spots, and are master evaders that escape predators with long, quick zigzagging leaps.

While the leopard frog is found in similar habitats to pickerel frogs—grassy fields and meadows along watercourses, often rivers and streams—it is less common than its closely related cousin. There are two ways to easily distinguish the two species. In the pickerel frog, the spots are rectangular and run down the back in two parallel rows, while the spots on the leopard frog are more rounded, surrounded by a pale border, and are randomly located along the back and sides. If you're still confused, you can look under the frog. If it has the orange wash on the ventral areas of the legs and abdomen, it's a pickerel, and if it does not, it's a leopard.

The base color of leopard frogs ranges from pale olive to brown. As with the green frog and bullfrog, there are rare instances when leopard frogs are blue. It is believed this is caused by the lack of surface pigment that normally absorbs blue light.

Leopard frogs emerge from their hibernacula as early as March. The males usually precede the females and set up shop along what are often the still-frozen edges of the water. When the water opens up, the breeding calls begin. The call of the male is a guttural snore, though, unlike the sustained snore of the pickerel, the leopard's call is given in a series of three-second groans, followed by a few short clucks. The call is not piping, as suggested by the species name of *pipiens*. This misnomer is the responsibility of German naturalist Johann Christian Daniel von Schreber, who, when he described this species in 1782, went by the accounts of a field observer who most likely heard nearby spring peepers and attributed them to this frog.

Mating generally takes place between April and June. The female lays up to six thousand eggs in an oblong mass attached to submerged vegetation, or on the pond floor. The eggs hatch within two to three weeks. The tadpoles, like most tadpoles, remain relatively sedentary, clinging to nearby vegetation or the egg mass for the first few days. They are brown, spotted herbivores that collect in groups to graze on algae. In most parts of the Northeast they leave the water within two to three months, but in northern areas they may overwinter as tadpoles and emerge late the following spring or in the summer.

Once the froglets develop, they spread out to the meadows and grasslands where they are active day and night, but mostly at night. These habitats provide them with the mainstay of their diet—crickets and grasshoppers. The breeding season is one of the few times to find adult leopard frogs in the water.

By mid- to late October, they are thinking of turning in for the winter. They do so buried beneath the mud of nearby ponds, lakes, and streams.

Northern leopard frogs are found in all of the northeastern states, but are not common. They are listed as a species of Special Concern in Connecticut. Their numbers seem to be declining in much of their range. Theories on why this is occurring abound, including habitat loss, agricultural practices (leopard frogs share their habitat with livestock), and acid rain. It is believed that while acid rain does not directly cause amphibian deaths, it increases the vulnerability of the amphibian to a host of viruses and parasites.

•

The **Southern leopard frog** (*Rana sphenocephala utricularius*) is very similar to the Northern leopard frog, but can be distinguished from its cousin by a pale dot on the center of the tympanic membrane. It also has fewer markings along the sides, smaller spots, and a more pointed head. Populations on Long Island and in a couple of isolated locations in lower New York state warranted its mention in this book.

Wood Frog
(*Rana sylvatica*)

Of all the frogs in our area, the wood frog is my favorite. Perhaps it is because I have encountered them more than the others. They are terrestrial dwellers of deciduous (and sometimes coniferous) woodlands. Perhaps it is because their quacking choruses in late winter signal the onset of a new amphibian season. It could also be that cool mask on their faces.

Wood frogs range in color between dark brown and creamy gray. They have a pair of strong dorsolateral ridges and a dark mask around each eye. They emerge from their underground burrows in late winter/early spring, looking very much like the dead leaves they traverse to get to the nearby vernal pools. Their species name, *sylvatica*, as well as their common name of wood frog, suggest the habitat in which they are most often found—the woods.

Like spotted and Jefferson salamanders, wood frogs are vernal pool obligate species, meaning that they require these temporary pools of water for breeding. It is not unusual to find them sharing the pools with those salamanders. The males typically arrive first, in March, and call while floating in the water. They have paired vocal sacs that expand from the sides. Their call is most often described as quacking or chuckling that can, and has often been, mistaken for that of a duck. The call begins at night but at the peak of the season can also be heard during the day. The females swim nearby and dive under the surface when ready to mate. The male, or sometimes several males, will follow a female and latch onto her back to fertilize her eggs as they are laid.

The eggs number from a few hundred to a couple thousand, and are held together in a clear, round gelatinous mass attached to aquatic vegetation. The mass is similar in appearance to that of the spotted salamander, which often can be found in the same pool. They can be distinguished by the surface texture: In the wood frog's egg mass, you can see the rounded outline of each outer globule, while the outer surface of the spotted salamander's egg mass is smooth.

Over time, the wood frog egg mass loosens and floats to the surface in a wide mat. This allows more of the embryos to collect sunlight, which aids in the development rate. An alga also grows on the mass, which serves two purposes: The oxygen given off by the algae feeds the embryos (whose carbon dioxide feeds the algae); and the algae is a ready food source for the newly emerged tadpoles, which stay with the egg mass for a few days after hatching. Hatching occurs in about three weeks.

The tadpoles develop rapidly. They are pure black at first, but then turn dark brown mottled with gold flecks. The rapid development is in response to the ephemeral nature of their aquatic habitat; they must complete transformation before the pool has dried. Their rate of development is dependent on how much water is in the pool, but they are generally on land within two months. The young froglets, miniature versions of the adults, stay by the pools for a short time to finish the job of absorbing their tails. By early summer they have dispersed into the surrounding woodlands, and are known to travel distances of twelve hundred feet from the breeding pools.

The rest of the summer and early autumn are spent in these upland areas, often a good distance from water. Wood frogs are primarily active at night, but can be found during the day as well, especially during periods of rain. They overwinter beneath the leaf litter, sometimes in shallow burrows, and are subjected to freezing temperatures, but as with the spring peeper and gray treefrog, sugars in the blood protect their organs from cellular damage caused by freezing. This allows them to inhabit areas even within the Arctic Circle, making wood frogs North America's most northernmost amphibian.

Wood frogs are common and are found in all of the northeastern states.

❧ 9 ❧

Finding These Things

IF YOU WANT to find frogs and salamanders, find water. The water can be sitting in a lake or pond, meandering down a streambed, or seeping up through the soil. Because amphibians require a good soak now and then, they can often be found in the water or within the vicinity. While some species, like toads, wood frogs, newts (efts), and redback salamanders do wander a good distance from water, that distance is only substantial in relation to where a set of little legs can take them. (For us, it's rarely more than a fifteen-minute walk away. And that's only for the long-distance travelers.) When vernal pool species lose their aquatic habitat to the thirsty trees and drying sun of summer, they seek out other wet places. In fact, any wet place in summer is going to act as a magnet for a number of amphibians as well as reptiles, insects, birds, and mammals. All living things need water, and it only stands to reason that that's where they will be found when it is in shortest supply.

I should clarify that by water, I mean fresh water. Salt does to amphibians what it does to slugs. It desiccates them. While some species, like Fowler's and spadefoot toads, can be found along salt-water shores, they still breed in pools filled by rain. The rest of the species are found inland.

Cover is another important element to consider when looking for amphibians. Most frogs and salamanders are active at night, when the air is damp and cooler. There are also fewer avian predators to contend with once the sun goes down. Many amphibians ride out the day beneath logs and rocks. Damp logs are best because they help keep the creature's skin moist, aiding in respiration. I cannot walk past a log without rolling it over for a look-see.

Believe it or not, there are rules for rolling logs. First, it's good to get into the habit of rolling the log toward your feet. In the Northeast there are relatively few venomous creatures that can be a danger to us, but as you get out west and down south, logs and rocks can play host to a handful of dangerous critters. Many, upon exposure, will seek to get away via the path of least resistance. If you roll the log away from you, they'll head right to your feet. If you roll the log toward you, they go in the opposite direction. In New England, yellow jackets are the biggest concern. Their subterranean colonies are like active land mines. Quite often, the entrance to their nest is beneath a log that is not sitting too tightly against the ground. If you roll the log toward you, you may buy an extra second or two for your getaway. It's amazing how quickly a person can move when spurred on by angry hornets.

Copperhead snakes and rattlesnakes do range as far north as southern New England, and both can be found under rocks and debris. While I have never come across one while flipping logs and rocks, I am always aware of the possibility. (To be honest, I would be thrilled to find one.) I have come across a number of other snake species while flipping rocks and logs. Most common are the ringneck snakes, which enjoy a good meal of the redback salamanders that share their habitat. I've been bitten by ringnecks, but only when I've picked them up. The bite is harmless and feels no worse than a pinch. Their primary defense is to release a foul-smelling musk. The musk, not their bite, is what I would prefer to avoid; it's an awful smell. But again, you'd have to be handling one to get slimed.

After you roll over a log or flip a rock, it is always a good practice to put it back in the position in which it was originally found. There can be a myriad of creatures residing beneath its shelter, benefiting from the moisture, shade, and safety from predators. Imagine yourself sitting at the dinner table when all of a sudden the roof of your house disappears. After the initial shock, you would go into a frenzy of action to avoid whatever it was that lifted the roof. And you'd much prefer that your roof was put back in place as soon as possible.

If there is nothing under the rock or log, putting it back is no problem. Gently roll it or place it down. If it's a rock, especially a good-sized one, don't let it thump to the ground; you could be caving in all sorts of tunnels beneath it. Will it kill the makers of those tunnels? Probably not, but replacing the rock gently can avoid a lot of rebuilding.

When there *is* something under there—a frog, salamander, snake, or mouse—you don't want to squash it when you put back the log or stone. If it appears that this is a possibility, you can nudge the creature out of the way or pick it up before replacing the shelter. If you have opted to pick it up, place it right next to the log as soon as it's been rolled back. I sometimes throw some leaf litter on top of the displaced critter for added protection, although I realize that it will probably return to its shelter shortly.

One of the most frequently encountered woodland amphibians is the red-back salamander. It is not unusual to find several sharing the same shelter. I've also come across mole salamanders, newts, and the occasional frog. Sometimes you don't know what you have in your yard until you give them a place to congregate. If you don't have a lot of logs or flat rocks in your yard, you can put down pieces of plywood. It might look like you are just littering, but they do get used by little ground dwellers that happen to be passing through. I am always amazed at their knack for finding these shelters. A while back, Betsy made cement stepping-stones for our yard. They are the size and shape of large rhubarb leaves, which she had pressed into the cement for a pattern. When Betsy makes something, she goes into mass production mode, so we had all these stepping-stones with no real place to put them. I placed a bunch of them at the edge of the yard, where the lawn meets the woods. I have found both redback and lead-back salamanders under these little shelters in all but the coldest months. The Carolina ground crickets love the stepping-stones, too, and it's often the first place I find them in the spring.

A great way to find some of the Plethodons is to flip rocks along a stream's edge. You can start with the flat rocks along the banks, again replacing the cover after you've checked for occupants. You will often find salamanders under the partially and fully submerged rocks along the bank, too. Flipping rocks in the water, however, kicks up a lot of silt, which reduces visibility. Also, salamanders are very quick in the water and difficult to catch for a closer look. I always try to anticipate their escape route. Very slowly lift the submerged rock to keep down the turbidity, and place your hand—or better, a net—where you think the surprised salamander will exit. The first thing it will attempt to do is wriggle beneath the nearest cover. If it accomplishes this, good luck in trying to catch it.

A net can be a useful tool for catching amphibians, and there are a variety of them out there that work well. The main thing to keep in mind is that the mesh needs to be fairly tight. One of those cheap butterfly nets you can pick up in department stores works fine. It's easy to bend the round hoop into a rectangle, which is a better shape for working streams. I bought one of my favorite nets at a pet store. It's designed for catching large aquarium fish and is small enough to tuck into a fanny pack and large enough to catch any amphibian I come across, including mudpuppies. One of the advantages in using a net is that you avoid handling the animal—

more on that shortly. The main advantage is that it gives you a bigger target in which to corral the animal. I find it easier to drive a submerged, or partially submerged, salamander into a net than to grab it.

Often, though, I am netless, in which case my only option is to make a grab for it. If the salamander is swimming away, and it probably will be, I remember my father's advice about passing a basketball. He would say, "Lead the ball," which meant throw it to where you think your running teammate will be rather than where he is now. If you grab for the wriggling salamander where it is, you'll end up with just a handful of palm; you have to aim for slightly ahead of where it's going.

The species you are most likely to find along a stream edge are two-lined and dusky salamanders. You will often find more than one under a rock, and sometimes both species will be side by side. While two-lined salamanders can be quick in the water, catching a dusky can be like grabbing a little eel. They have a laterally flattened tail, which makes them good swimmers. They also tend to burst away from danger, putting their all into getting as far as possible from trouble the moment that danger presents itself. This doesn't require them to travel a great distance. Usually, as soon as they get themselves wedged beneath the closest rock, they stop moving. The same can be said for the other streamside salamanders, the two-lined and the spring.

Two-lined salamanders employ an interesting defense strategy when on land. They flip into the air, writhing and lashing about. I would imagine that in addition to startling a predator, this makes them tough to grab.

Speaking of grabbing, never hold or catch a salamander by the tail. Many, such as the blue-spotted, four-toed, and redback salamanders employ tail autotomy. The tail can break off at the base and continues to move on its own. The predator is left with a meal to keep it distracted while the tail's former host slips away. The tail eventually grows back. Feel free to grab any frog you can by the tail, though. If you can accomplish that feat, you are in a class of your own.

•

Some salamanders, such as the slimy and spotted, exude a sticky secretion when threatened or handled roughly. This renders them unpalatable to most creatures. You don't want to stress them to the point of having to sweat toxins. Helping a salamander or frog across the road on a rainy night could be considered necessary stress, however. For a few seconds of its life, a large predator has caught it, and then it's free again, with an exciting story to tell the grandchildren.

Holding an amphibian for a long period of time is generally unnecessary. You may do so to either transport it to a container for further study, or to get a better look at it there in the field, but bear in mind that this action can be deadly to the animal. Human skin secretes acids and salt. Since amphibians breathe through their skin, they are highly susceptible to *our* toxins. Our hands can be even more toxic when covered with soap residue, perfume, hand creams, or insect repellent. Whenever possible, I will dip my hands in water or rub them on damp moss before picking up a frog or a salamander. If this is not possible (but it usually is), I just make it a point to handle the creature as little as possible.

Also, always wash your hands *after* releasing the animal. You would be surprised how often your fingers end up in or near your mouth and eyes. This is especially important after handling amphibians with noxious skin excretions such as toads, mole salamanders, and slimy salamanders. While the toxins won't kill you—at least not the ones produced by species in the Northeast—they can irritate your eyes and mouth. And they taste extremely bitter. Trust me, I know. After I helped spotted salamanders cross a street a few years ago, I slid into my car to write down the name of the street I was on and then put the pen in my mouth. I can tell you that a spotted salamander tastes like chicken—chicken that's been sitting in the sun for three days.

Washing your hands after picking up a frog or salamander is also extremely important to protect the animals themselves. Wild amphibians are always at risk of exposure to infectious disease through contact with their moist environment and other amphibians. When you handle one amphibian after another, you increase the chance of spreading a whole variety of pathogens not only to the individual amphibian you have touched but also to the whole population of amphibians it will later be rubbing elbows with. This risk is even greater if you are traveling from one area to another. Biologists recommend wearing disposable gloves and changing them between specimens. Even plastic bags can be used. If you do not wear gloves, your hands should be washed with antimicrobial soap or cleaned with alcohol wipes. Be aware of open cuts on your hands, too. There are many bacteria living in these moist habitats—salmonella, campylobacter, and a whole host of other things to make us sick. What is present in that habitat can be expected to be present on its denizens.

It's also possible to spread amphibian pathogens from one habitat to another via your muddy boots. To be honest with you, I do not disinfect my boots when I go from one site to another. Have I wiped out any amphibian populations as a result? I doubt it. While cars allow humans to travel to more areas in less time, I rationalize that these creatures have had all manner of other intruders—birds, mammals, insects, and reptiles—passing through their habitat over the centuries. Many have dipped their feet in other ponds prior to their arrival at a new one. I'm just one more animal passing through. I do wash my hands, though.

Along those same lines, you also do not want to put individuals from different populations in the same container prior to sending them back into the wild. When you release them, they should always go back into the *very same* pond, lake, and stream where they were found.

•

Up to now, I've covered mostly salamanders. Finding frogs can present different challenges. Some, like the leopard and pickerel frogs, can be found in lawns and meadows. Toads and wood frogs are not uncommon on the forest floor. The same can be said for peepers, which can also be found along the edges of pools. The rest are going to be in and around water.

Frogs tend to be a little less secretive than salamanders. While I have found many species beneath rocks and logs, it is not with the frequency that I find them in other, less hidden, habitats.

Sometimes the frogs find me. One of my hobbies is watching moths. To attract them, I hang an ultraviolet light in front of a big white sheet. The moths come to the light and land on the sheet, which offers me the opportunity to see what's out there and to take some pictures. But I get other visitors as well. It is not unusual to see any number of frogs along the bottom of the sheet or clinging to its surface. Many wood frogs, American toads, spring peepers, gray treefrogs, green frogs, and pickerel frogs have me to thank for an easy meal of moths. It's as if I set the table for them and rang the dinner bell. I am always torn about what to do when this happens. Do I let them eat these bugs I'm trying to have a look at? Do I take them away after what had to be like winning the lottery for them? I end up alternating my actions, and the decision usually has something to do with which group of animals I'm feeling more well-disposed toward on that evening.

I should mention that I don't run the light every night. Artificial light can have a detrimental effect on nocturnal animals. I make sure to leave the black light off for long stretches of time so the critters can go about their business without interruption.

Check your porch lights, too. Because the lights attract insects, the frogs are often not far behind. The same goes for windows, which are also areas of concentration for nocturnal insects. It's always a treat to see a treefrog sticking to a window, and it's an opportunity to see the inside workings of an amphibian. When a treefrog clings to a window, its belly is pressed tight to the glass. If you hold a light to it, you can see through the translucent skin and observe the stomach, intestines, and pumping heart. Because frogs swallow their food whole, there could also be a hapless bug working its way down the pipes.

A gray treefrog attracted to bugs at a porch light

•

While these are examples of the frog coming to you, what's more fun is for you to go to the frog. A number of years ago, Betsy gave me what may hold the distinction of being the best Father's Day present I've ever received— chest waders. I'd wanted them ever since a certain January afternoon when I saw some guy floating around in a pair on Cedar Lake in the town of Chester, Connecticut. His waders were surrounded by an inner tube, and I imagined that instead of boots, he was wearing small fins. Beside him was a floating cooler attached to his waders with a short cord. (I don't know what was in his cooler, but I do know what *I* would have had in there.) So, Betsy and I drove by this man, bobbing up and down in the gentle lake currents, fishing pole in hand, floating cooler alongside. It was late in the day, almost twilight, and he was the sole figure on the decent-sized lake. I said to Betsy, "Oh, my God. We are looking at the happiest man on this planet."

The next June, I got my neoprene waders. They don't have the inner tube, but I can still get to some incredible places. In my opinion, there are three reasons to wear waders: They protect your feet from sharp objects and give traction on slippery, moss-covered rocks; they keep you warm in the cold water; and they keep the leeches off you. Where leeches aren't a problem, a pair of neoprene scuba booties are all you need for ponds and stream edges. Some people wear scuba suits instead of waders, and some wear jeans and sneakers.

You have to be mindful of sinkholes and the potential for getting wedged in submerged logs and rocks. It's a good idea to carry along what I call a poking stick to prod the area where you are about to step. If you poke the floor and the pole keeps going, you might just want to skip that pond entirely. You should also be careful not to disturb eggs or egg masses; it's best to stay out of the ponds while the eggs are still developing.

You can expect that anything you have with you will at some point get wet. As careful as you are with your camera or binoculars, even they will dip into the water. I keep mine handy, but in a waterproof case. There are many great photo opportunities from this perspective.

July. I am chest-high in a pond in northern Vermont, looking for mink frogs. I have about an hour, maybe an hour and a half, of light left. The pond is an overflow area of a large woodland lake. It is filled with lush vegetation, and tussock-lined channels snake off in all directions. I put on my waders and enter that little bit of heaven.

I search the edge of the pond for mink frogs, but don't find a single one. There are plenty of adult and newly metamorphosed bullfrogs, though. Green frogs call from just beyond the next patch of vegetation. I call back. I have had luck in the past with getting this species to respond; it requires a fairly decent simulation of part of a Spike Jones bit—a guttural twang coming from the back of the throat.

Dragonflies and damselflies hunt along the edges—maybe that explains the surprising lack of mosquitoes. I find myself wading into the maze of channels; one leads to another, which then forks into two more. Caught up in traveling these lanes, I completely lose track of time. The sun is just tapping the tops of the trees when I turn to head back.

It is then that I notice where I am—all alone in a pond by a lake in the woods. No houses for miles. No dogs barking. Just the sounds of twanging green frogs, chittering swallows, and insects humming. I think of the guy floating in his inner tube waders on that late winter afternoon.

I don't find any mink frogs, but sometimes, the hunt is the thing.

Catching a frog in the water has to be done with a net. If it is floating on the surface, you slowly slip the net into the water and bring it up from beneath the frog. This way, as soon as it senses danger and dives, it goes right into your trap net. On land, your hands are usually all you need. For the smaller species, all you have to do is cup your hands around it. Don't be surprised if the frog decides to christen you; urinating is a defense mechanism and, as with the oozing salamanders, is a sign of stress.

Larger frogs require a different technique. There are a couple of ways to pick them up. One is to grasp their shoulder blades (or scapulae) with your thumb and forefinger. Another way is to grasp it—again, gently—around the hips. Wrap your thumb and forefinger around the point where the legs meet the body.

You want to be very careful not to squeeze too hard, especially in the abdominal area. Because of the danger in hurting the frog with a grip that's too strong, I recommend *not* wearing heavy gloves or work gloves. It is too difficult to sense the pressure you are applying, and one tends to overcompensate. A damp paper towel or surgical gloves work well. Remember, if you use your bare hands, make sure they are wet and that you clean them in between handling different individuals.

If the frog is a female and obviously filled with eggs, just leave it alone, or if you absolutely have to pick it up, use a net.

When handling the frog, be careful that you don't allow it to slip from your grasp and injure itself by falling to the ground. Most frogs are designed to land from jumps they can perform under their own steam, and the height of a standing human can exceed that distance.

I rarely find it necessary to handle a frog anymore. These animals have enough stress in their lives, and I prefer not to add to it. If I must pick up a frog, I do so for the minimum amount of time needed—that is, unless I want to show someone how I can hypnotize it. If you turn a frog on its back, it remains motionless as if asleep. Sometimes, you can help this along by gently rubbing the frog's belly. Once it's "under," you can actually open your hand and it will continue to lie still. (At this point, you want to be careful what you say because the frog is now in a highly suggestible hypnotic state. Once, thinking I was being funny, I told a hypnotized pickerel frog that it was a dog. I can't begin to describe how bad I felt when, shortly after, I observed the frog running after a cat. When the frog caught up to the cat, it quickly, and sadly, learned that it was most certainly not a dog.)

How to hold a large frog

A "hypnotized" pickerel frog

I'm not sure why frogs are rendered immobile this way. I do know that in the wild, frogs are never found on their backs. Not only is this a highly vulnerable position, but a frog also has absolutely no reason to be in this pose. I wonder if the response that kicks in—the appearance of lifelessness—is akin to that of an opossum or hog-nosed snake playing dead when it feels threatened. Most predators prefer to have done in their own prey; it assures freshness. And which would be more likely to fool a predator, a frog that is consciously keeping still or one that is genuinely knocked out? I would guess the latter. If I had a grizzly sniffing and pawing at me, it would be much easier for me to appear dead if I really were unconscious, and the struggle to keep from flinching or making a noise would be greatly reduced.

Have you ever read the *Ripley's Believe It or Not!* entry that featured a frog pumping iron? This sideshow act was actually very easy to accomplish. The only tough part lay in finding a set of tiny barbells. Once those are found, or made, the frog is put on its back and the weights are set in its

Living Room Salamanders

Cindi and Bill Kobak's terrarium is something I look forward to seeing every year, but can never count on. It's a large undertaking, and some years, they just don't get around to it.

The terrarium is about as close to a small pond habitat as can be created indoors. They start it off with scoops of pond water and soil, which seems to explode with life once the soil settles. Tiny ostracods, copepods, and daphnia glide jerkily over the bottom. Apple-green hydras plant themselves along the glass sides. Rocks, sticks, and other detritus are added to mimic the natural conditions. As time goes on, various creatures come and go. Dragonfly nymphs split their skins and emerge as dragonflies. Salamander larvae lose their gills. Various worms and other invertebrates feed and are fed upon.

You can watch this incredible little ecosystem as if through a cross-section of a living pond. What makes it so fascinating, I think, is that we are accustomed to looking down at these things and don't normally see them from a lateral view. This perspective seems to offer a more intimate look at the subject.

The salamander larvae in Bill and Cindi Kobak's terrarium are fed with mosquitoes raised in a rain barrel. The salamanders are released before they are fully developed. BILL KOBAK PHOTO

hands. The frog, in attempting to push away, or in this disoriented state, right itself, lifts the weights in the air.

It's amazing the little distractions the human mind can come up with.

I'm not going to spend much time on housing frogs and salamanders. I have never been that keen on taking things from the wild, especially for the purpose of keeping them as pets. I think the best place for an animal to spend its life is in its natural habitat. I sometimes make an exception, though, when it comes to tadpoles and larvae of common species. The individuals you take are probably gaining an edge in survival (providing you take good care of them) because predators have been removed from the picture. As long as they are returned to where they were found, there should be no real negative impact.

I have been known to borrow the occasional amphibian from the wild once in awhile. For example, a few years ago, I wrote and illustrated two children's books, *A Wood Frog's Life* and *A Salamander's Life*. Each follows the life cycle of the title character from egg to laying eggs. In order to get my reference for the paintings, I really needed to rear them out. In each case, I found an egg mass and kept it in a plastic aquarium filled with water from where they were found. As the eggs hatched and I got my reference, I released the larvae into their natal pond, keeping just a few in the aquarium.

Keeping frog tadpoles fed is easy. They graze the algae found naturally on the submerged rocks and vegetation or on their egg mass. They also feed on detritus and their fallen brethren. I even tried fish food, which they ate, and boiled up some lettuce, which they also seemed to like. When the algae source got low, I introduced algae-covered sticks and leaves. It is a good idea to observe what the tadpoles are feeding on in the wild. There are many different algae, and not all of them may be suitable for your tadpoles.

Mole salamander larvae, being carnivores, are kept fed by adding at regular intervals scoops of water from the pond and leaf litter from the floor. Both elements contain all kinds of little invertebrates for them to feast on. This does offer the potential for throwing some predators into the mix, but fortunately, that did not happen when I was raising my salamanders. It is important that you check your aquarium for diving beetles, water scorpions, and other insects that prey on salamander larvae and tadpoles. As the tadpoles grow larger, you can feed them brine shrimp purchased from a pet store. Or, go scoop some mosquito larvae from a pond. Trust me; the mosquitoes will never make it out alive.

As with any aquarium setup, you should keep an eye on the water quality. The number of creatures living in the tank will dictate how frequently the water will need refreshing. If it starts to get cloudy, scoop out as much as you can (you don't have to empty it completely) and replace with newly acquired pond water. Waste and uric acid build up very quickly in this relatively small enclosure, with fatal results.

•

When the larvae and tadpoles get further along, I provide them with a place to haul out. The transformation from water to air breathers does not happen in a single instant. As the gills are absorbed, the larvae make more and more trips to the surface. At some point, you may notice that they are keeping their heads out of the water longer than they are keeping them submerged. Juvenile salamanders and froglets stick very close to the water, keeping some part of their body submerged.

For frogs, food is not a concern at this time because they are transforming from herbivores to insectivores. To ease the transition, nutrients are provided by the tail, which is slowly being absorbed. Salamanders are a bit hungrier when they leave the water and will eat any of a number of little creatures living around the pond's edge.

It is at this point that I usually release them. There are times, however, when I need to hold on to an adult for a little while—when it is a species I know friends would like to see or when I need to get a photograph. If I don't have my camera when I come across an interesting subject, I may capture it and bring it home. I then either take the pictures in my yard or back where it was found.

I really do make a point to return every animal I borrow back to the exact place from where it was kidnapped. Sometimes it's a chore and it's the last thing I feel like doing the very next day and it would be so much easier to slip the salamander or frog into my own pond, but I don't. I've established my own code of ethics, which allows me to rationalize taking the occasional animal from its natural habitat. The code says the animal must be returned to its place of origin within twenty-four hours. For one day, my captive is sidelined from action. Following that, its life goes on unimpeded by this curious human.

Because they are not going to be permanent pets, the accommodations I provide are spartan and serve to meet the temporary residents' needs. I usually grab some leaves, wet them, and place them in the glass or plastic container. I find the little plastic terrariums sold at pet stores to be the best for holding amphibians. They come in an assortment of sizes and can be stored one inside the other, making for more room in what can be a very crowded supply bag. It is very important that the added leaves are wet, and I try to add enough water to create a small puddle at the bottom, just enough to allow them to submerge their belly.

Salamanders will go right into the leaves, burying themselves as best they can. Frogs aren't as secretive. When frightened, they may jump excessively and can traumatize themselves by hitting the container's lid. Using a deep opaque cage or container will minimize the trauma. You can also put a towel over the container to settle them down.

As mentioned earlier, you should not mix different species, or even individuals of the same species from different areas. This can spread disease, and toxins given off by one amphibian could be harmful to another. For example, if you put a peeper in with a pickerel frog, which is poisonous, you end up with a dead peeper. You should always clean out the container between uses, too.

I truly believe that the best place to observe these animals is within their own element. To see a green frog in an artificial container is taking it out of context; it's a frog with the background removed. To see that same frog, sitting at the edge of the pond looking like he owns the place, is a far more rewarding experience.

❧ 10 ❧

Create It and
They Will Arrive

THE PHRASE "build it and they will come" has been so overused, but I tweaked it a bit for this title anyway. The truth is, you can construct an amphibian habitat, and if you have frogs and salamanders in your area, they will find it. I've done this on both a large (bulldozer) and small (shovel) scale and have seen it done with great success by others.

Many of us already alter our yards to make them more wildlife friendly. We plant flowers for butterflies and fruit-bearing trees and shrubs for birds. We hang feeders and nest boxes, maintain meadows and copses, and leave brush piles for cover. The key is to provide what the target animals need to survive, or at least supplement what is out there. There are precious few places where good habitat for wildlife is actually on the increase. The reality is that once a house or building is constructed, it is there until it either falls or burns down. Then a new one is built in its place. It stands to reason that if one cannot fight the inevitable, efforts made to lessen its impact can go a long way.

You can actually make your little microcosm a place where wild things can gain sustenance. Think of Central Park in New York City. This patch of green in the middle of a busy metropolis has attracted a quarter of all the bird species in North America. A bird passing through is going to be drawn to this area because it offers that which cannot be found in the surrounding area. It becomes a wildlife magnet. If you have in your yard what does not exist elsewhere in your neighborhood, the wildlife that is still hanging on along the outskirts, or passing through, will find you. Even if good habitat does exist in the vicinity, you can still count on visitors from the adjacent communities. Ideally, one would want his or her neighbors to join in the effort, creating a bigger net to draw in that wildlife. The National Wildlife Federation has been encouraging this for more than thirty years with their Backyard Wildlife Habitat program. They offer information on how to make your yard a little wilder, and they certify your yard when it's completed. Tens of thousands of people have participated across the country. I would imagine that if all those yards were combined, they'd make for a sizable sanctuary.

•

Making your yard more attractive to amphibians inevitably involves creating a place that holds water. In addition to attracting frogs and salamanders, human-made ponds are also attractive additions to the landscape. If you currently don't live on waterfront property, you can change that.

A good place to begin is to see what you already have on and around your land. If you find frogs in the grass or salamanders under logs, they must be coming from somewhere. Find out where. The question would then be, can you improve on what already exists? It is often the case that the amphibians in your yard came from habitat in someone else's yard, or from nearby open space. Amphibians spread out from their natal ranges to colonize new ones. Actually, that is the way of all living things. Range expansion is a key to survival. While it is important to provide areas where they can safely pass through, or linger until breeding or turning in for the winter, it can also be helpful to add to the network of potential breeding areas. Even if they don't breed in the pools you created, the habitat can still serve as important rest stops for amphibian travelers.

Once you decide you want to create a pond, you have to determine whether it will be for vernal-pool species or for amphibians that need water throughout the year. In the case of the former, you have to be careful that you don't inadvertently build a trap for the herps that will be utilizing the pool. If you make a pond that invites them to lay eggs, but the pool continually dries out before the eggs have a chance to develop, you are just making things worse for them. These are called sinks or egg dumps. They do occur naturally, but are often in areas where other, viable pools also exist. In fact, satellite pools inconsistent in their ability to facilitate the amphibian life cycle surround many vernal pools.

Some towns require that you get a permit before making a pond, and most, if not all, would require it if that pond is planned in existing wetlands. You may even have to go through the Army Corp of Engineers if the activity is going to take place on a classified wetland or if you are going to divert an existing watercourse. While to you, it sounds like a positive thing that you are doing, the town conservation department or inland wetland commission may want to be assured that what you plan to do won't have a detrimental effect on existing wetlands. It is the onus of the home-owner to check the local regulations and make sure that he or she is acting within them. The local commissions will let you know if your project has to go to an agency beyond them. Be prepared to show what you plan to do, where you plan to do it, and what you hope to accomplish. Most commissions would like to see a scale drawing of the pond in relation to the lot. A cutaway showing the depth could also be required. You will most likely be adding native plants around the edge, and a list of those plants, with an indication of where they would go, may be called for as well. The level of detail required will vary wildly from town to town. Many officials will want to conduct a site walk of the area in question before rendering a decision. It would be a good idea to have the site marked off with string to show where the pool is going to be built.

Now, all of this is assuming you plan to build a sizable pond. If you are just putting in what many would call a water garden, something say, three to six feet across in the middle of a non-wetland area, this is less of a big deal. It gets more complicated in larger projects involving heavy machinery. But even those little water gardens can make incredible frog ponds. The first one I made was only about four feet by three feet, situated on my front lawn by my studio window. Over the years, I documented

A little frog pond with a liner. CINDI KOBAK PHOTO

The author's little pond, filled with gutter and curtain drain runoff

breeding wood frogs, spring peepers, and spotted salamanders in there. It was also visited by bullfrogs, green frogs, pickerel, and gray treefrogs, not to mention all the birds and mammals that stopped by for a dip or drink (or amphibious snack). It is this kind of pond I will be focusing on in this chapter, because just about anyone can build it without having to jump through all kinds of regulatory hoops.

•

If all you want is to make a little pond in your lawn, you should select an area that will be suitable for the amphibians in your community. A location in partial shade is a good compromise for most of the creatures. A pool in direct sun will be better for aquatic plants, but the summer sun will suck that thing dry in no time. A pool in the shade will stay filled longer and the leaves will continue to fuel the food chain. The rule of thumb is to replicate as best you can the conditions of a functioning pool. Have a look at pools producing new amphibians in your area. Many will be in places where there are at least a few trees around them. The exception is the spadefoot and Fowler's toad habitat, which is often in the sand and out in the open. Their toadlets can develop quickly enough to be gone before the water disappears.

If you don't have trees, then you can plant some, or put in some native shrubs. This is especially important if you wish to entice spring peepers, which gather in the low branches around ponds in the spring. I made a little pond on my current property that attracts peepers and other amphibians. Night by night in the early spring, you can hear them calling in the woods as they get progressively closer to my pond. When they arrive, there is no mistake they have landed. They ring in the warmer weather as they peep day and night for about two to three weeks. What a treat to the ears.

If the pool is intended to be vernal, that is, dry during the summer months, it will have to be in an area that already holds water long enough to get the amphibians through the breeding cycle. This may require doing some digging in wetlands, which, again, will most likely be regulated by your town and possibly by the state. However, the location also could be at a low point in your yard where water collects after moderate to heavy rains. This may not be a registered wetland, and therefore is probably not regulated.

You can divert water from gutters to the pool area. That last pool I created is kept filled through most of the months by water running through curtain drains around my house and under my driveway. While one cannot be expected to install drains just for this purpose, many houses already have them, so why not make use of the diverted water? There is a new movement in the gardening world that utilizes drain water. They are called rain gardens. Water from roof gutters is channeled from the down-spout to a low-lying area in the yard. That low area can either be created, or may exist naturally, and is planted with flora that like wet feet.

Check the soil before committing to a location. If it is sandy or gravelly, it would probably not suffice as a natural vernal pool. If it is made up of clay, it may hold the water once a basin is created. Dig down to different depths—one, two, and three and a half feet—and grab a handful of the dirt. If it can be flattened and holds its shape at approximately the length of your palm, you have some pretty good clay that may hold the water. The deeper the clay level is, the better. If there is gravel just beneath the clay, there may be some future leakage problems.

●

For a small, water-garden type pond, you're better off using either a pre-formed or flexible liner. These can usually be purchased in gardening or landscaping stores. You can also shop around on the Internet. Some people I know have used concrete to line the pond. While it works for a while, it has a tendency to crack and leak. If it is a small enough pond, it's no big deal to fix, but a larger one would require that you destroy the habitat you created to get at the problem area. Clay is also used as a basin, but has the same disadvantages as cement. I have always used either the natural substrate or a flexible liner, which gives you the freedom to make the pool any shape you'd like.

One thing you want to be sure about when choosing a liner is that it will not leach toxic chemicals and petroleum byproducts into the water. Just because it's plastic or rubber and holds water does not mean it will be suitable for a pond meant to support life. Some materials that look like they'd be perfect for a little frog pond may have been designed as roof coverings or tarps. Look for a liner intended for use in koi ponds, as these will be fish safe. They are usually made from PVC or propylene. For your purpose, a thickness between twenty and forty-five millimeters would be required. It should also be UV-resistant, as sunlight is a liner's biggest enemy.

There are many brands out there to choose from, so do some shopping around for the best price. You should expect the liner to last between twenty and thirty years. The thicker it is, the longer it will last. However, thicker liners can be more difficult to work with, especially in cooler weather. They can also be quite a bit more expensive. The initial cost should not be your only concern, however; avoiding the possibility of having to rebuild a pond after the liner has begun to leak is worth whatever extra money you spend at the outset.

It's a good idea to have the liner available before digging the hole. Of course, this means that you have to know how large the pond will be before you order the liner. You can use a garden hose or a rope to lay out the shape on the grass or dirt before you begin digging. Try and go for a natural shape rather than a perfect circle or oval. My goal is to make the pond look like it was always there. I love the laying out stage of the project. It's one hundred percent visualization. You have this little squiggly hose on the ground to represent what you see in your mind's eye as a wet and verdant Eden filled with all manner of primordial creatures. Your hands are still clean, and your back is still straight (no muscle spasms yet from all the digging). There are only two aspects of pond making I enjoy more than this, and I'll get to them shortly.

•

Then comes digging time. First, make sure you are not digging where there is a water or power line. I've seen too many Three Stooges movies to make that mistake. You can always call your utility company if you are unsure of where the lines are. Digging a hole in the town of Killingworth, where I live, is a nightmare. Shovels hide behind the other tools in the shed, fearing they will be called upon once again to break through the layers of stone and clay we call soil. You may be luckier in your vicinity.

The depth of your pool should be determined by the freeze zone in your area. In Connecticut, for example, one could expect that a depth of two and a half to three feet at the deepest point will make it through the winter without freezing. Bear in mind that you will be adding some fill to cover the liner, and you will want to allow for that. Assuring that the deepest portion will remain unfrozen encourages some of the true frogs, such as green, leopard, and pickerel, to overwinter in your pond. Try to keep that deeper part somewhat flat. This will not only make it easier to work from within while you are sculpting the edges, but it spreads out that nonfreezing zone, preventing creatures from having to pile up in the middle.

The sides of the pool should slope gently upward from the center. The rim should also be level from one side to the opposite side. You may have to shave off some of the edges to accomplish this. You can also tier some sections. Shelves at different levels around some of the perimeter allow for plants that require different water depths. They also create different temperature zones for the developing eggs and larvae of frogs and salamanders. The shelves should be at least a foot wide for added stability and to leave room for marginal plants, which may or may not be kept in pots. Avoid creating a steep drop from the edge of the pool. This could make it difficult for creatures to exit when the time comes. Birds will also drop in to drink from the shallow edges.

Once the hole is dug, tamp down the soil as best you can and line it with newspapers or carpet for padding. Dampening this prelining material will make it easier to keep in place. You can also purchase a commercial geotextile pad. This will protect the liner from the roots and sharp rocks beneath it. Once the hole is lined with some form of padded layer, it's time to drag in the liner. Hold off any trimming until it is in place—you can always cut it smaller, but you can never cut it bigger. Pack the liner down, working from the center out, and leave plenty of it overlapping the edges of the pool. Once it is in place, cover it with the dirt that was excavated from the hole. (Some suggest putting another protective layer of textile fabric over the top of the liner first. That's probably a good idea, but I've never done it.) About three to six inches of dirt cover is good. This will provide a natural substrate for plants, tiny animals, and overwintering amphibians. It also protects the liner from UV light. When the dirt is in place, tamp it down with your feet and hands.

.

And now for my second-favorite part of the project. You will need three items to really do this right: a hose, a lawn chair, and a cold bottle of beer. Place the end of the hose in the center of the pool and turn it on. (If you put it at the edge, it may wash down some of the soil you have packed against the liner.) Plant yourself in the lawn chair and crack open the beer. I cannot stress enough the importance of that last step. If you are not a beer drinker, substitute your beverage of choice. Watching the water rise in that big hole you dug is one of those moments in life that is meant to be savored.

Once the pond is full, turn off the hose and let everything sit for at least two days. This will ensure that the liner has settled into place. Now it's time to trim the liner that was left hanging past the edges. Trim it down to about two feet outside the perimeter of the pool. It's better to have too much extending beyond the edge than too little. The pond may settle over the years, bringing the liner down with it. If the liner pulls down too close to the edge, rain and snow can get underneath it and create pockets, and the liner area over those pockets will be prone to cracks and leakage.

Some people stake down the edges of the liner, which is not a bad idea, but I just cover it with dirt and rocks. The goal is, again, to have it look natural. Covering up as much liner as possible also reduces its exposure to UV light and prevents water from getting underneath, both of which can cause damage.

.

Part of the fun in making these little pools is the landscaping. Look at the plants growing in the ponds in your area to see how well they are doing and where they are growing. Some are submerged, some are partially submerged, and some grow in the damp soil along the edges. There are other plants, such as duckweed, that float on the surface.

More and more landscaping stores sell aquatic plants. I prefer to stick with native species. Betsy, however, likes to garden with cultivated plants. This has been a source of arguments between us for about a quarter of a century, and we usually just agree to have our own sections of the yard to do with what we wish. With our first pond, however, we both put in an equal amount of work, so that was not an option. I argued that I wanted it to look like a wild pond. She argued that it was right next to her flower gardens and there is nothing wrong with having a few attractive cultivated plants growing in it. I won the argument, or at least I thought I did. Her plants have a way of appearing in places where they weren't before, and our first pond was no exception. What continues to amaze me is that I have never once caught her in the act, which leaves her with a thin thread of deniability of which she takes full advantage.

Betsy did come up with a great idea for planting in the pond, though. For the water lilies, she took some old stockings and filled them with pond dirt. Then she stuffed in the root, and tossed it in the middle of the pond. She also did this with a number of the plants along the edge. This not only prevents the roots from growing into the liner, but also makes it easier to remove dead or unhealthy specimens without disturbing the pond floor. A few plants we set in planters, and some, with shallower root systems, went right into the dirt. We bought a few of the plants and some we relocated from other ponds (with permission from the property owner). The advantage in transplanting from an existing wild pond is that you get all the little critters that come with the soil.

I like to line the edges with moss found elsewhere in the damp woods on my property. You can peel a section off a rock, dip it in the pond water, and lay it on the pond edge. To hold it in place on the slopes, drive some sticks into it (unless you are using a liner). My friend Bill Kobak painted some of the rocks in his yard with a mixture of the moss and beer. You get a handful of moss and mix it in a blender with a cup or two of stale beer, or buttermilk, and spread it on the rocks or logs. Once the moss establishes itself, it keeps growing on its own.

•

My *favorite* part of the project is what I call "hamburger helper." Wild ponds, be they vernal pools or permanent bodies of water, are teeming with life. Much of that life is so small that it requires a microscope or magnifying lens to observe. If you scoop a jarful of water from a pond and hold it up to the light, you will see tiny crustaceans—ostracods, copepods, daphnia, and others—darting jerkily about. Scoop up a pile of leaves from a pond floor, put them in a white pan filled with water, and you'll find even more—worms, isopods, various larvae, planaria, and too many other tiny fauna to mention here. These are the base of the aquatic food chain; these ~~what make the pond alive; and these are what you want in your pond.

; bucket and a net and find a pool in your area that is similarly
/our own. Fill the bucket about halfway with water from the

pond. This will give you some of the creatures that remain suspended in the water. Then scoop up a bunch of the leaves and soil from the bottom of the pond and put it in the bucket. Do this until the bucket is full, and then dump it in your pond. You have now activated it with life. A large pond will take more buckets, and, to increase the diversity, I suggest you take from different areas of the wild pond. You could even take from different ponds.

In most cases, the new pond will become self-sufficient as a result of that initial introduction of creatures. Granted, not everything will successfully establish itself in your water habitat. What will survive is what your pond will support. Over the years, as your pond becomes self-sufficient, you could supplement it with scoops from other ponds to add some variety. Just be aware that what you add could be detrimental to what is already there. The animals, bacteria, and fungi will cycle through the seasons as they would in a natural pond.

The larger creatures, if not present in some form in your introductory buckets, have an amazing knack of locating these little pools. Soon, water beetles, dragonflies and damselflies, mayflies, midges, and caddisflies will find their way to the new habitat. So will mosquitoes. This is a good thing, because their larval and pupal stages are food for many other insects as well as for the amphibians. You don't see a lot of adult mosquitoes making it out of these habitats. They have greater success in standing water in tires, tree holes, children's pools, and wet places not harboring insectivores. Vernal pools can be thought of as natural mosquito traps.

Because a pool contained in a liner is not affected by the water table, it is technically not a vernal pool. It will stay filled throughout the seasons. (Granted, you may have to top it off with the hose now and then to assure this.) However, from an amphibian's perspective, it can offer the same advantage that a vernal pool does, *as long as you do not add fish*. Many fish eat amphibian eggs.

I would like to make an important suggestion: Do not put goldfish in your pond! I know it will be tempting for some. Here's another one Betsy and I battled over for years after making our first pond. She wanted koi. I wanted frogs. Every once in awhile I would find a shiny orange fish in our pond. People who have koi or goldfish ponds are always looking for places to unload surplus fish, and Betsy had a hard time turning them down. I won in the end, thanks to the hungry raccoons passing through and the mysterious trail of marshmallows leading from the woods to the pool. (No, I would never have done that.)

If you have a larger pond, one made by a bulldozer, for example, you *can* have coexisting fish and amphibians. It is important that you first provide them cover in the form of logs, rocks, and plants on the pond floor. I still would not recommend adding nonnative fish. If you want an outdoor koi or goldfish pond, that's fine. Just make sure that pond is not also creating an attractive nuisance for native amphibians. They have enough predators trying to eat them without us introducing new ones. Find a way to keep the natives from entering the pond and wasting their eggs by feeding them to your exotic fish.

Someone once asked me what I thought about introducing native frogs and salamanders to an artificial habitat. If none are already available in the area to colonize the new pond, my gut feeling is that it's probably not a good idea. For one, you would be taking the individuals away from a place where they belong. While they may do well in your new pond for a while, they have no place to spread out to. And if they don't spread out, you end up with a pool crowded with banjo-playing inbreds. But they will spread out. It's in their nature to do so. Where do they go if yours is the only habitat in the area?

If there is good habitat available to them outside of your yard, then bringing in species from other areas can spread disease in the form of viruses, fungi, and bacteria to the native populations. It is best to be patient and let the local amphibians find you, and they will.

•

While I have spent most of this chapter describing the creation of little ponds, larger ponds can be made the same way. The difference lies in the tools required. Instead of a shovel, a bulldozer is needed to excavate. If the area does not have a high enough water table to keep the pond filled, you can use a liner. It's going to be a big liner, though, and very heavy, so you will need some people to help you roll it out over the depression. Instead of newspapers or carpet to line the bottom, you can use a couple inches of playground sand.

Some ponds are created by diverting water from a stream or river. Watercourse diversion usually falls under the aegis of the Army Corps of Engineers. While it sounds intimidating, it can be worth your while to pursue this, so long as you are not having a negative impact on the existing wetlands. Don't worry; the Corps will see to it that you don't. A great resource for anyone building larger ponds is *A Guide to Creating Vernal Ponds*, by Thomas R. Biebighauser. You can get it through the USDA by calling

(606) 784-6428. It is lavishly illustrated and takes you step by step through the whole process. Just looking at the pictures makes you want to build your own pond.

Regardless of the size of the pond you create, you can add to its effectiveness as an amphibian habitat by providing cover along its edges. Once a frog or salamander leaves the water, it seeks cover to avoid drying out. You can place logs and large, flat stones around the perimeter to help them out. Not only does this give the frogs and salamanders shelter, it creates habitat for the insects, worms, and crustaceans they feed on. It also makes it easier for you to find them.

I hired someone to bulldoze a pond for me at my last house and created a thirty- by forty-foot vernal pool in an area where the water table was high and the clay was thick. It was adjacent to existing wetlands, so our inland wetlands commission saw this as a positive wildlife enhancement to the area and approved it. While the pond was butt-ugly for the first year, by year three, you would have never known it was man-made. For the most part, I let the surrounding flora fill in where it wanted to go. I also added wetland edge plants like buttonbush, spicebush, turtlehead, and native rushes and sedges. In the shallow water along the edges, I planted water plantain and pickerelweed. In the deeper parts, I added water lilies. These were all plants that could be found in the vicinity, and they thrived in this new habitat. Betsy's idea of putting the plants in stockings made it easier to install them in the deeper areas. It was just a matter of tossing them into the middle of the pond.

It wasn't long before bullfrogs, green frogs, spring peepers, wood frogs, pickerel frogs, American toads, gray treefrogs, and spotted and marbled salamanders discovered the pond. Four-toed salamanders could be found under rocks along the edge. This was all on a piece of land not much larger than an acre and a half. What made it so successful was its proximity to wetlands in our neighbors' yards.

I did run into some trouble one particularly dry year, when the pond level went down before the gray treefrog tadpoles had a chance to develop. I caught as many as I could and moved them to our smaller water garden pond in the front yard. With their brick red tails, these are the most attractive tadpoles you can come across. I felt somewhat responsible for their dilemma because I had created the habitat that sold them short. They completed their metamorphosis in the little pond, and by mid-summer the surrounding plants were adorned with little, green, grape-sized froglets.

I had the opportunity to revisit the pond a couple days ago. It is now on its second owner since we moved. The woman who lived there right after us was deathly afraid of frogs, which I learned at the closing. We sat around the table, signing papers, and I was telling her and her husband about the six species of frogs and four species of salamanders their new property would be playing host to. As I talked, her face twisted into a mixture of fear and disgust while her real estate agent gestured wildly for me to stop talking. "What?" I asked. "She is afraid of frogs," the agent said. I looked at Betsy, confused. I couldn't even imagine a person being afraid of frogs, especially a person choosing to move into a rural area. "They're harmless," I said. "Ugh, I just hate them," the new owner said. Luckily for my slimy little friends, that family only lived there a short while. Maybe she really did hate frogs that much, because in the meantime, they disassembled my (okay, *their*) natural water garden, put in a preformed liner, and stocked it with fish. God only knew what happened with the big pond in the yard. My curiosity got the better of me a few days ago, and I gave the current owners a call.

The author's old bulldozed pond, eight years after it was built

Mike and Maura, to my relief and delight, love amphibians. When I asked for permission to come see how the pond was doing since it was built, she was shocked to hear that it was man-made. "We thought it was always there," she said. Seeing it for myself, eight years after its creation, I can understand why they thought that. Aside from the berm on the western side, created from the removed material, there isn't a clue that it was dug out by a bulldozer. Maura told me that her friends didn't believe her when she described how hundreds of these big salamanders with yellow spots filled the pond and then disappeared after a few days. She took them out at night with flashlights to prove to them that she wasn't seeing things. She was so excited to have the salamanders visit and to listen to the calls of the frogs in the spring.

Hearing this made my day. I couldn't be happier, knowing that not only the amphibians, but also their new stewards are appreciating the pond.

•

I love the fact that we can actually have a positive impact on our surroundings. All too often we hear about the bad things we do to natural habitats. And we sure do some bad things, some very bad things. However, with just a bit of effort, we can change that which was once destroyed into a sanctuary for those chased away. Your yard is your canvas, and you can choose the scene you wish to create. Granted, compromises may have to be made if there are two artists painting the picture. Fortunately, while Betsy and I may have a different style and approach, we both love frogs. We want them in our yard, so we are sure to paint them in. For us, the greatest reward comes on those spring and summer evenings when our little microcosm on this planet is filled with their song.

ᔥ 11 ᔥ

Save the Salamanders!

FIRST IT WAS "Save the Birds!" and then it was "Save the Whales!" Somewhere in the middle of all that was "Save the Snail Darters" and "Save the Baby Harp Seals!" Who would have ever thought we'd be hearing "Save the Salamanders"?

Hey, I'm all for saving birds, whales, fish, and seals, but I would never have expected salamanders and frogs to be at the forefront of a movement. Okay, frogs maybe, because people have always liked frogs, but those slimy nocturnal lizardy things? And maybe the word *movement* is too strong, but more and more groups of people *are* getting together to fight for their survival. Many worldwide organizations are devoted to securing a place for amphibians on our planet. To name just a few here in the United States, we have: PARC (Partners in Amphibian and Reptile Conservation); ACA (Amphibian Conservation Alliance); DAPTF (Declining Amphibian Populations Taskforce); Frogwatch USA (no fancy acronym); and NAAMP (North American Amphibian Monitoring Program). Even our federal government is involved. President George W. Bush and Congress directed the Department of the Interior to "initiate a national program of amphibian monitoring, research, and conservation." Thus in 2000, ARMI (Amphibian Research and Monitoring Initiative) was created as a branch of the U.S. Geological Survey.

What has activated this interest in amphibians is the evidence of their overall decline on this planet. Countless areas once hosting healthy amphibian populations now have fewer, and in some cases, *no* frogs or salamanders. Some of us can recall seeing species a few years back, such as the Monteverde golden toad and gastric brooding frog, that are now believed extinct.

Scientists all over the world have studied the reasons for this decline. As I described in detail in the "Canaries in the Coal Mine" chapter, they lay the blame on the usual rogues gallery—climate change, habitat loss, ultraviolet radiation, pollution, disease, fungi, and predation by nonnative species. They believe that there is no single reason for the overall drop-off in amphibian populations and that the cause is most likely a little from column A and a little from column B. A habitat already stressed by alien predators will fall more easily at the onset of disease; a population of frogs fighting the effects of increased UV light will be more susceptible to pollution, and so it goes.

Because this is a worldwide concern, it takes the cooperation of people across the globe to stem this onslaught against our herpetofauna. It is equally important that people know what's going on in their *own* area. Our home territory is where each of us can have the greatest impact, both negative and positive. For most of us, armchair conservation is the only practical way we can help beyond our community. We send in our checks and let the recipients of our support do the work, but unless we live near that rain forest or coral reef, we don't get to experience hands-on the results of our involvement. Knowing that we contributed financially has to suffice, and, fortunately, for many of us it does. However, when we act on a local level, we can actually drive by or even visit the area we took part in protecting. There is great satisfaction having played a role in shaping our neighborhood, which in essence, is an extension of our own backyard.

In addition to the national organizations mentioned above, smaller amphibian conservation groups can be found in just about every state. A quick list that covers the Northeast would include the Maine Herpetological Society, Vermont Herpetological Society Online, New Hampshire Herpetological Society, Rhode Island Herpetological Society, New England (formerly Massachusetts) Herpetological Society, and the New York, Long Island, and Western New York Herpetological Societies. In 1998, Connecticut added its name to the list with the formation of the Connecticut Herpetologists League. It's interesting to note that these groups focus on amphibians *and* reptiles. The two classes seem destined to be forever linked.

A good number of people are interested in herpetoculture, which is the keeping and raising of herpetofauna as pets. One of the advantages to having a club populated with members who actually rear the creatures their club is focused on is that they tend to have a greater knowledge of the biology of those organisms. Their interest doesn't end with a checkmark next to a name on a life list.

The fact that there are organizations out there to share in and foster the enjoyment of amphibians and reptiles comes as no surprise to me.

What does excite me is the fact that more and more laypeople who are becoming interested in preserving our herpetofauna. By laypeople, I mean
those who may never have even seen a spotted salamander or a wood frog,
but nonetheless show up to town meetings to speak on behalf of saving the
amphibians' habitat. Granted, a number of those people are NIMBYs
("not in *my* backyard") who couldn't care less about amphibian habitat. For
them, the frogs and salamanders are a tool to prevent development in their
immediate vicinity. However, some who begin that way ultimately become
converts when their eyes are opened to the real-life wonders residing in
their and their neighbors' yards.

Public hearings are where those aforementioned clubs come in handy.
They can provide expert testimony and a unified voice when attempting
to persuade those in power to consider the fate of the amphibians when
voting to allow or reject development in their habitat.

So what can people do? First, find out what needs to be done. Are
vernal pools being filled in your town? Are they being used as storm-water
basins? Are developments installing curbs or silt fences that impede amphibian migration, or putting in frog-swallowing storm drains along a migration route? What is the minimum upland area of review around
wetlands and watercourses in your town? Are local businesses or industries
discharging water, clean though it may *appear*, into your rivers and
streams? Are the last remaining open spaces becoming fragmented by new
communities? These are just some of the many practices and conditions
that threaten the well-being of not only amphibians, but also a wide variety of native, and nonnative (you know, most of us) fauna and flora.
These are things we should care about.

A great place to start is to educate yourself on the functions of the various arms of your town government. Find out who actually has the au-
thority to do what needs to be done. With regard to the protection of
wetland and watercourse habitats, the town conservation commission or
the inland wetlands and watercourses commission would be the agency
stepping up to that challenge. The charge of the latter is to regulate and
minimize any and all disturbance in wetlands (areas with wet soils) and watercourses (areas with standing water—streams, lakes, vernal pools,
etcetera). That's all they can do; anything that takes place beyond the wetland areas is outside of their purview.

Town conservation commissions tend to have a wider scope. In addition to regulating wetlands and watercourses, they can work with the other

town offices in preserving open space, wet and dry, protecting rare or beneficial wildlife, keeping town parks clean, and educating the public on the value of doing so. Planning and/or zoning commissions, to put it simply, deal with where buildings go and how many can fit in a given area. They would also be the ones to determine how much open space, if any, would be preserved within that development. Many towns require open space to be set aside to mitigate the loss of wild areas taken up by developments. For example, in my town, any development larger than twenty acres must have at least fifteen percent of that area designated as open space. In theory, that open space should have some value as open space. In actuality, it is usually wetland habitat that cannot be built on anyway.

Planning and zoning can also, to a degree, deal with light pollution issues. Excessive artificial light is a growing concern not only for those who wish to see stars in their neighborhoods but also for those who care about the nocturnal fauna and flora. A recent study showed that redback salamanders sleep later when their habitat is inundated by artificial light. These animals are likely to be among the most numerous vertebrate insectivores in a given area. One has to wonder what can happen as a result of one of the top predators sleeping in on a regular basis.

●

Vernal pools have become a hot-button topic in many areas throughout the United States. Up until fairly recently, they were considered puddles that could be filled in without a second thought, but now most states recognize them as watercourses and bring them under the jurisdiction of the state and town agencies that deal with these habitats. That said, many towns are still not up to speed in adding vernal pool protection measures to their regulations. Vernal pools need to be delineated from the other watercourses because the reasons for their protection differ. Most watercourses are regulated because of their value as watershed rechargers and suppliers of clean drinking water. They also provide hydrological stability, flood and erosion control, and wildlife habitat. Vernal pools do play a role in recharging watershed areas and providing erosion control, but their highest value lies in their importance as wildlife habitat. They are the sole habitats of a number of dependent or obligate amphibians and invertebrates. You fill in the pools with dirt, and you lose these animals.

Now, here's the tricky part. Once you recognize that the value of a vernal pool lies in its designation as sole habitat for dependent species, you have to take it a bit further. Many of the amphibians that utilize vernal pools do so only for breeding and larval development. Following breeding and egg laying, they spend the rest of the year in the surrounding woods. A change in that surrounding habitat can greatly reduce the value of the pool. Trees are also vital to fueling the energy in the pool. They regulate water temperature and are responsible for keeping the pools vernal in nature because, in summer, their roots suck them dry. The water is stored in the trees to get them through the winter. Prior to that, the leaves offer shade, which cools the water and can reduce excess algae growth. The leaves that drop into the water in the fall become food for bacteria, fungi, and various invertebrates, and are the first link in the food chain.

So, when you set out to protect vernal pools and the species within them, you also need to protect the upland area surrounding them. How much do you need to protect? Well, consider this: Spotted salamanders will take up residence within about a 350-foot range around the pool. Jefferson salamanders will go about another 100 feet. Wood frogs are the real travelers, spreading out 1,500 to 3,500 feet from the pool's edge. An average of 750 feet is generally used as the critical terrestrial habitat needed to preserve the amphibian denizens of vernal pools. The distance varies with the size and depth of the pool as well as the surrounding topography. If you were to draw a circle with a 750-foot radius around a pool, it would encompass a huge area and likely end up encroaching on neighboring properties and even towns. I think it would be unrealistic to require landowners to keep that much area undisturbed. Make that *impossible*, because it would never stand up in court. So, what do you do? Four things, and in this order: inventory, educate, lobby, and follow up.

Inventory

Think the lyrics from "Big Yellow Taxi": "Don't it always seem to go, that you don't know what you've got 'til it's gone." It's hard to preserve something you don't know exists. It's a good idea to know where the vernal pools are in your town. One place to begin is to ask your conservation commission or inland waters and wetlands commission if the pools have been mapped. In towns that have already done their homework, the maps should be available at the town hall and the town clerk can tell you how to go about finding them. (Incidentally, town clerks are one of a town's most valuable resources. They may not have all the answers to your questions, but they can always point you in the right direction.)

If the critical amphibian habitats have been mapped, look at where these wetlands are located. Ones in existing developments are pretty much a done deal. If some exist in open space, are the stewards aware of them? If not, they should be, and if pools are in public open space, they can even be used for education.

Your concern should lie with the vernal pools located in tracts of land that may be targets for development. You want to keep tabs on those parcels and make sure your planning and conservation commissions do right by them if building projects do get approved there.

Most towns *don't* have their vernal pools mapped. You could either encourage the members of the commission to take that on or volunteer to do it yourself. By yourself, I don't mean just you, as a force of one. This is a pretty big job, and the more people you get aboard, the better chance you have of completing the project. Maybe the local land trust or one of your state herp groups will join the effort. Ideally, you will get someone from your town conservation or wetlands commission involved. For one thing, he or she (or they) can make sure that what you identify as a vernal pool meets their commission's definition of that habitat. You'll also have a friendly ear should you or your group ever have to lobby the commission on a future concern. This representative will have participated in the process and can share that experience with the rest of the commission.

To start off, you need to look at maps—assessor's maps, U.S. Geological Survey maps, and any other topographical map showing wetlands in your town. Another good resource is recent aerial photos. Many towns have them. The pictures are usually taken when the leaves are off the trees, and on good-quality images, you may be able to locate the pools as little dark circles. You then have to figure out where those pools lie in reference to property boundaries, which is where the tax assessor's maps come in handy.

The next challenge lies in getting permission from private landowners to walk their land. To truly certify that you have a bona fide vernal pool, you need to field test it. Some owners get nervous about this, fearing that if you locate a vernal pool on their property, they will be limited in what they can do on their own land. Be as reassuring as you can, but in some cases you'll just need to chalk it up as one you couldn't get to.

Criteria vary from state to state and town to town. Find out what your local government defines as a vernal pool. Here are some helpful resources in the Northeast that cover what these states consider a vernal pool and how to certify them as such:

Connecticut—"Vernal Pool Wetlands of Connecticut" is available from the Cooperative Extension System Bulletin Room at the University of Connecticut (www.canr.uconn.edu/ces/forest/pub.htm).

Massachusetts—"Wicked Big Puddles, A Guide to the Study and Certification of Vernal Pools" by Leo Kenney is available from the Vernal Pool Association (www.vernalpool.org).

New Hampshire—Refer to "Identification and Documentation of Vernal Pools in New Hampshire" by the New Hampshire Fish and Game Department's Nongame and Endangered Wildlife Program (www.wildlife. state.nh.us).

Maine—"Maine Citizen's Guide to Locating and Documenting Vernal Pools" is available in PDF format from the Maine Audubon Society (www.maineaudubon.org).

While I couldn't come across printed formats for New York, Vermont and Rhode Island, a Web search will turn up helpful pages. In fact, all of the northeastern states have a lot of information online. If you do not have access to the Internet, ask someone who does to print that information for you, or stop by a library, many of which are hooked up to the ether world. You can also get a copy of your town's regulations from town hall.

•

Another way to determine where vernal pools are is to go out on those first rainy nights of late winter and early spring and observe where the obligate species are migrating. Where are they headed and where are they coming from? Indicator species are the best guides for finding their homes. I've discovered a number of pools I did not know existed by coming upon spotted salamanders or wood frogs crossing the road. Listening for calls works, too. The sound of wood frogs coming from the forest is a sure sign of vernal pools.

The North American Amphibian Monitoring Program has been surveying the country for years. If your neighborhood has not yet been covered, you can initiate that effort through a local nature center, club, or land trust, or simply get some friends together and have fun. NAAMP regional coordinators train volunteers on how to identify local amphibian species by their calls. They also explain when and how to conduct the survey and provide materials such as a thermometer and a training CD or tape of the frog calls. Each group or solo volunteer is assigned a roadside route. The survey is conducted several times during the calling season to catch the early- through late-breeding species.

I did this a few years with some friends. We'd head out, listen for frogs, and end up at a pub, which, somehow was always included in our route. You can contact NAAMP at their Web site: www.pwrc.usgs.gov/NAAMP.

Once you know where the pools are, or even concurrent with finding them, education is key to their protection.

Educate

If you don't know where the habitat is, or even if it exists, you of course can't protect it. If you *do* know where it is but people don't care that it's there, you'll still be fighting an uphill battle if that habitat becomes threatened by development. So, how do you make sure people start to care about protecting these habitats?

It's not always easy, but fortunately, once people learn about these little self-contained ecosystems in their own backyards, many *will* start to care very much about them. The private property owners who get nervous about letting people find vernal pools on their land are the people you hope to sway first, because they can probably get away with doing whatever they want to their vernal pools. Mind you, legally they cannot, since most towns protect these habitats, but the reality is that probably no one will know if they choose to fill in a vernal pool or clear around it. Conservation commissions and zoning/wetland enforcement officers do not run surprise inspections of people's backyards. Unless Mrs. Kravitz is peeking through her curtains next door, people can pretty much do what they please, undetected, within their property boundaries. If you can convince a number of landowners how fortunate they are to play host to these incredible habitats, then you've taken a huge step in securing the future of thousands of small lives.

One way to do this is to facilitate lectures on local amphibians and their habitats. A number of people offer them; some speak for free and some charge up to two or three hundred dollars. Your local land trust, conservation commission, nature center, Audubon chapter, local or state herpetological society, or a combination of any of them can sponsor these talks. They should take place in a public place and should be free. You want to reach as much of the public as you can, and some will be turned off if they have to shell out even a minimum amount of cash. Make sure the talks get publicized in the local print and broadcast media by providing press releases and photos/illustrations well in advance. Scrape together a budget so you can buy ad space in the newspaper, because free listings in the community calendar section are not always reliable.

The best place to find speakers is by talking to the groups mentioned above. Many who write about frogs and salamanders offer slide or Power-Point lectures to help spread the word and incorporate their talk with a book signing. People like to go home with something. Many lecturers also bring in live specimens to show the audience. I generally don't like live animal presentations because the animals always seem distressed at being in a room filled with staring predators (us). In these situations, however, I tend to make an exception because people will care more about these frogs and salamanders if they actually get to see them up close and personal. A picture may be worth a thousand words, but a live marbled salamander or spotted salamander, or a few tiny peepers, can be worth a thousand pictures. They are real crowd pleasers.

Since nothing beats seeing the real thing, you also want to get people's feet wet. There has to be a vernal pool somewhere in your area where the public can be brought to experience firsthand what they have to offer. There's nothing like watching fairy shrimp dancing in the dappled sunlight or seeing the gelatinous masses of eggs sitting on the floor of the pool or pools. Water scooped up in a clear jar will reveal tiny copepods, ostracods, and daphnia, which are in essence, wild "sea monkeys." Dredging up some leaves from a pond bottom and sorting through them in white pans could turn up all manner of crawly things—damselfly nymphs, isopods, caddisflies, fingernail clams, and my favorite, green planaria. It's always a good idea, too, to point out how many of these creatures feed on mosquitoes.

While there are usually a good selection of naturalists in your region qualified to lead these forays, why not train yourself to do it? People think you have to be an expert to lead a nature walk, but that isn't true. It can be satisfying to learn together. If you scoop something out of the water and don't know what it is, look it up with the group. When you find it, you'll share in the satisfaction of discovery. And isn't discovery more fun than being told something?

There are some great field guides out there, and more keep coming. One of the best for vernal pools in the Northeast is *A Field Guide to the Animals of Vernal Pools* by Leo P. Kenney and Matthew R. Burne. It's full of crisp photos of many of the things you can expect to find in these habitats. A new book just out called *Vernal Pool, Natural History, and Conservation* by

Elizabeth A. Colburn, while not a field guide, covers basically everything you would want to know about the biology of these bodies of water. It's the kind of book you would want to read before setting out. Other guides are mentioned in the back of this book, and I think it's always a good idea to have a number of different books on hand for cross-referencing.

If you schedule a series of visits, you can watch how the pool changes as the season progresses. You can see its denizens go from eggs to tadpoles and larvae to juveniles. Watching something develop from the egg can add an element of empathy, which is what you want to elicit. It's easier to eat a chicken from the supermarket than one you've watched progress from a chick. Remember, you need to get people to care about these creatures.

Naturally, much of this will be preaching to the choir. Many of the people who turn out to these programs already care about such things. But they may not know a lot about them. In fact, many may not have seen a salamander or fairy shrimp or wood frog. What you are doing is increasing the knowledge base within your community. You'll need to have that community behind you when you seek to sway town officials to do the right thing. And just maybe, one of those people who tramped along on a vernal pool field trip will someday notice someone filling in a vernal pool and will talk to that neighbor about it and perhaps sway him or her to respect the town regulations that protect these habitats.

Lastly, there is one more resource at your disposal—the media, both local and regional. Invite a reporter to join you during the salamander migration. For many of them, it sounds like such a bizarre thing; they come along because it would make an interesting story. You can also write articles for the local paper. Editors are always looking for local interest articles about any aspect of your community. You, or someone else, can write up a number of articles for them pertaining to your local frogs and salamanders. Whenever possible, include pictures.

Lobby

Quotes heard at hearings:

"You're putting salamanders before people?"

"Who are *you* to tell me what I can do in my yard?"

"I've made vernal pools before, and I can tell you the *lizards* that use them don't need *that* much area around them."

•

Emotions can run high at public meetings. You hear a lot of things said just for the sake of scoring points. Some people just like to hear themselves speak. Others think hearings are venues for venting about everything that's happened in town during the past decade. What the officials holding the hearing are actually looking for are data to support whatever decision they make. When the issue in question involves amphibian habitats, an excellent resource for such data is *Best Development Practices: Conserving Pool-Breeding Amphibians in Residential and Commercial Developments in the Northeastern United States*. Authors Aram Calhoun, PhD, and Michael Klemens, Ph.D., filled their book with scientific evidence based on case studies of what amphibians need to survive in and out of the water. They also make recommendations on what towns can do to protect these creatures. If you become an intervener—that is, if you choose to try to stop or alter a development because of real threats it poses to a wetland habitat—it will help if you study this book, make copies of the pertinent passages, and share these with your commission. The factual information in this book will give you firm footing in what is often a mucky area.

Many towns have incorporated Calhoun and Klemens's recommendations into their town regulations. For example, some towns require a buffer, or upland review area, of 500 feet, 600 feet, or 800 feet around vernal pools. (Most, though, specify between fifty and one hundred feet.) While the towns probably cannot prevent all activity from occurring in those larger areas, they can require applicants who wish to develop their property to show the vernal pools on their site map. Many pools that would have otherwise been missed get picked up this way. What the commission can do is attempt to steer the activity away from these areas. They can also dictate the manner of erosion control. Silt fences and hay bales are the most frequently used structures for preventing silt, which is stirred up by the removal of natural erosion controls, from running into the nearby wetlands. This is all well and good, but, they can also impede amphibian migration. Many town commissions therefore require that the fences be staggered when adjacent to a vernal pool. This allows the animals through while still stopping the silt.

The reality is that most commissions will not be able to regulate activity more than 100 or 200 feet away from the edge of the wetlands. To go farther than that would require that they prove the activity will still have an effect on the pool itself. For a good number of vernal pool habitats, that's a challenge. With a larger review area, you at least get a bigger picture of

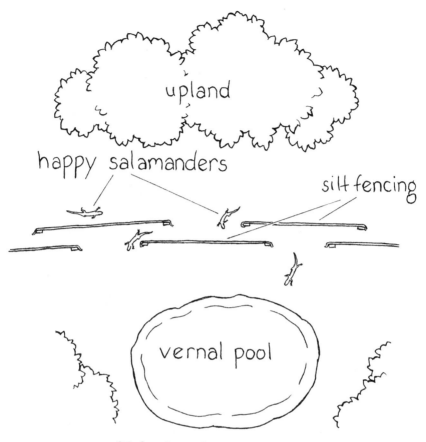

Silt fence layout for vernal pool areas

the overall habitat. Maybe a road can be diverted so it doesn't bisect a migration route. Maybe a few of the houses could be shifted to leave a larger undisturbed area of woods for the frogs and salamanders. It is often the case that these changes don't greatly affect the developer's profit margin. And some developers would prefer to create a community that promotes natural diversity.

It is important to familiarize yourself with state statutes regarding wetlands and vernal pools. The wetland regulators are bound by these statutes, which vary from state to state. These statutes change over time, so there would be no purpose in attempting to list them here. For example, Connecticut recently allowed upland review areas to be protected by virtue of the presence of obligate species in that area. A judge rescinded that regulation. Then the state government reinstated the rule by weakening it.

They said a wetlands commission could deny activity within upland (buffer) areas only when said activity threatens the physical characteristics of the pool itself. So, those obligate species were again protected, but only so long as they stay in the water! Personally, I think our government missed the point entirely. The value of a vernal pool lies in its function as a host to these obligate species. If you can kill them off while they're not in the water, you've defeated the purpose of protecting that pool. One government official described this new regulation as a dog chasing his tail.

But, who knows—the statute could change again. This hammers home the need to stay up to date on your state regulations. And if your town is falling behind, you can petition for a regulation change.

Having participated on both sides of the table, I can tell you that when the deliberation occurs, the discussion tends to focus on the specific issue before the board or commission. There is a reason for this. The denial or acceptance of an application for development can be challenged in court. If that decision came about as the result of something as empty as political party stances, for example, it stands a good chance of being thrown out in court. It doesn't look good for that commission to keep losing ground this way. It is also very expensive for the town to keep defending questionable decisions. A planning and zoning, wetland, and conservation commission must make their decisions based on fact, not emotion or political leanings.

Of course, this doesn't always happen. The men and women on these commissions got on them because they have an opinion on how they would like to see things run. We all say we have open minds, but on most issues, don't we all lean one way or another? Your success in making your case to a commission rests on your ability to bolster the opinion of the commissioners who already lean in your direction and to overwhelm those who don't with facts. The reality is that sometimes the latter cannot be accomplished.

It is incumbent upon the developer to prove to these commissions that what they are proposing will not have a detrimental effect on the wetlands. It is their burden. It is incumbent upon you, the citizen, to introduce evidence to the commissions when you see that what is proposed will have a negative effect. So, how do you do this?

You attend hearings. Many towns will hold a hearing if there appears to be significant activity in a natural area. Sometimes the commissions call the hearing, sometimes citizens petition for one. Prior to the hearing, a map and the proposal should be available for your perusal at town hall. Go look at where the homes or buildings are in relation to the wetlands. Are those little boxes that represent buildings sitting within those curved lines representing wetlands? If so, there's probably reason for concern.

Show up at the hearing informed, or bring someone who is. This is where one of those herp groups could come in handy. If they don't have someone in their organization who can help you, they can probably lead you to someone who can. You can't just show up at a hearing and say, "I don't like this because we are losing too many wetlands in town." Or, "I'm worried that you will destroy this wood frog or spotted salamander habitat." One of the least effective things to do is complain about "all the development going on in town." While maybe valid, these are just opinions, and commissioners need data and facts.

Avoid the use of the word *possible* when addressing impact. Anything is possible, and decisions cannot be based on a chance, maybe, that *perhaps* something could kind of possibly happen. You need to know, and be able to convince the commissioners, that there is a *probability* or *likelihood* that an undesired outcome will arise from a particular aspect of that development. Those are two very important words—use them if you mean them. They are the only words with some legal weight behind them. You need to have the facts and you need to present them in a manner that can be digested by the layperson, which many of these commission members are. Surprisingly few of them are biologists and naturalists.

Expert testimony is invaluable here. You, or your representative, will be up against the expert testimony provided by the developer's consultant, who has been hired to demonstrate to the commission that no harm will come as a result of their intrusion into or around the wetlands. Environmental consultants hired by developers to evaluate habitat and opine on the impact of a given activity can make recommendations to reduce that impact. If the developer decides to take the consultant's advice, it is incorporated into the plan that is put before the deciding commissions. You can count on the environmental consultant to testify at the hearing or presentation of the application to the commission.

If you don't feel that the applicant did enough to save the wetland habitat, it is that consultant you will have to best in the eyes of the commission. Remember, though, that the consultant could very well be right. You may not like what the development will look like, but from a wetlands standpoint, there may be no problem. Salamanders care not of scenic affronts. Frogs don't pay taxes. All they need is their clean water and ample space to spread out to dry land. If that is provided, you probably don't want to bring them into the argument.

Know that these consultants have credentials to back them up, too. Yes, they are obviously paid by the developer, and yes, they would not be retained if they spoke out against the development, but most commissions have to rely on the strongest evidence before them. If you think there could be a problem with the wetlands, but aren't sure, there is nothing wrong with asking questions at a hearing, or encouraging the commission members to ask questions of the expert consultant.

There are three factions at these forums: those who are for approving the application, those against it, and those who would like to learn more about it. If you strongly suspect there will be problems, do your homework, get the facts, and get someone with credentials on your side.

•

I should backtrack at this point, because it may sound like I am bashing developers. I am not. I'm not sitting outside in the woods typing this. I live in a house within a neighborhood that was built by a developer. Among my many jobs after college was building houses. Most people want to lock the door behind them after they move into town. Naturally, that's an unrealistic attitude. Destroying natural areas for homes is a necessary evil, but someone has to do it. Just as someone had to clear acres and acres of wild land to replace them with monocultures of nonnative fruits and vegetables for our consumption.

There are lots of responsible developers who care about preserving as much of the natural landscape as possible. Many contribute their free time and equipment to help conservation organizations. However, as with any faction of society, there are others who make their brethren look bad. These are the ones we have to do battle with within our towns and states. Why concentrate on developers when there are bad apples among the bankers, lawyers, cops, auto mechanics, and authors of natural history books as well? Because, by virtue of their career choice, they are in the position to destroy wildlife in our communities. They put the saw to the tree and the blade to the ground. When certain developers don't care about minimizing the effect on the natural area that is their canvas, it is the responsibility of the citizens within that community to seek a better outcome. (Those who watch these things happen and make no attempt to do anything about it have lost the right to complain.)

•

You should know that few developments are completely stopped because of environmental concerns. Some kind of compromise is usually worked out. Maybe the plan is scaled back and the developer puts in fewer homes or reduces lot sizes or simply repositions structures so they are farther from the questionable areas. Perhaps mitigation is offered. As engineering techniques improve in habitat restoration and creation, this solution is being applied more and more. Personally, I am not a big fan of mitigation. What usually happens is that one wetland is allowed to be compromised if the developer creates a new one nearby, or restores a different one that may have been impacted in the past. I see this as robbing Peter to pay Paul. You're still destroying a wetland or watercourse, a habitat that has likely taken many centuries to form. While it *is* possible create new habitat, it will not be the same as the one that was ruined.

That said, I have seen instances where mitigation was beneficial. In one case, a landowner wanted to build a house in an area surrounded by wetlands. The only way he could get to it was to skirt, and fill in, a section along the very edge. The town wetlands commission did not look favorably on this. A mitigation deal was offered: In order to be granted a permit to impact that twenty-foot strip, the owner would turn over more than twenty acres of his thirty-acre lot to the town's land trust. The commission agreed, and more than twenty acres became permanently protected as a result of sacrificing that thin ribbon of wetlands. Here, Peter was robbed to pay Paul, but Paul made so much that Peter got a kickback.

My point is that if you are really concerned about the welfare of the amphibians and their habitats, keep an open mind when considering solutions to protect them. If you are just hoping to stop development, chances are the frogs and salamanders won't help you. The only sure way to keep open land open is to own it yourself or work with organizations that buy and hold land for open space. But you *can* make a difference in amphibian conservation—a big difference.

Follow Up

The last step, following up, is important. Let's say the town did the right thing and protected the critical habitat you were concerned about. Let people know. Bad news travels fast. Good news can have a hard time getting out of the garage. Positive actions taken by town officials should be noted and commended. Most of these people, many of whom are volunteers, hear from citizens only when they have a complaint. If town officials know that people are watching what they are doing and will support their often difficult decisions, their backbones will be a little stronger the next time a similar issue is brought before them.

If a protected habitat is on public land, then monitor it and let people know that it is thriving. Education is an ongoing process. People leave town and new people move in. They may not have been here to witness the last go-around.

And lastly, serve on these commissions yourself. You may not have a chance to change the world, your country, or your state, but you can have some say in how your town is run. For the most part, we choose the town we live in, and we choose it for a reason. I chose my town for its rural nature because I care about the wildlife, I concentrate mostly on those areas. I want to hear the peepers peeping in the ponds and the toads trilling in the woods. I want to have to weave around crossing salamanders when I drive home on a rainy spring night. Fortunately, I'm not alone, and there are things I've been able to do, with the help of others, to protect that which is important to me. You are not alone, either, as you will learn once you get involved.

Glossary

Ambystoma – Short for Ambystomatidae, refers to a mole salamander.

amplexus – The embracing of amphibians for the purpose of reproduction.

Anura – The order of tailless amphibians known as frogs.

balancers – Lateral appendages on the heads of some larval amphibians used for stabilization while swimming.

buccal pumping – A method of respiration using the throat muscles.

bufotenine – The psychoactive chemical found in the parotoid glands of toads.

Caecilian – The order of legless burrowing amphibians. They are found in tropical regions.

Caudata – The order of tailed amphibians known as salamanders.

cloaca – The common chamber into the digestive, urinary, and reproductive canals.

congress – Cluster of mating salamanders.

costal grooves – Vertical grooves running up the sides of some salamanders.

desiccation – The removal of moisture.

detritus – Disintegrated matter, often referring to plant and animal matter, on the bottom of ponds and forest floors.

DOR – Acronym for Dead On Road, which refers to amphibian road mortalities.

dorsal – Top of the body.

ectotherm – Often referred to as cold-blooded, an animal that regulates its body temperature through heat exchange with its surroundings.

glucose – A simple sugar that acts as an energy source, and, in some cases, as antifreeze in animals.

glycerol – A sweet, syrupy trihydroxy alcohol used by some animals to survive freezing climates.

herpetofauna – Amphibians and reptiles.

herpetologist – A person who studies amphibians and reptiles.

hibernaculum – The shelter of a hibernating animal.

hybrid – An individual created by the mating of two genetically distinct species.

intraherpetofaunial glacier – The advancing ice crystals within frogs that freeze in the winter.

larva – The early stage of any of various animals that undergo metamorphosis. In amphibians it most often refers to salamanders, but can be used for frogs as well. Plural is larvae.

lateral – On the sides of the body.

nasolabial groove – A narrow slit lined with glands that runs from the nostrils to the upper lip—present in the Plethodontidae.

natal habitat – Place of birth and early development.

neotonic – Retaining larval characteristics.

otic notch – An opening in the skull behind the eye, covered by the tympanic membrane.

parasphenoid teeth – In amphibians, teeth located on palate.

parotoid glands – External, raised poison glands found on toads. They are often located on the shoulder or behind the eyes.

Plethodon – Short for Plethodontidae, refers to a lungless salamander in this family.

scutes – Protective plates.

spermatheca – A receptacle in the female reproductive tracts in which spermatozoa are received and stored until needed to fertilize the ova.

spermatophore – A clump or packet of sperm contained within mucoid material. It is produced by many species of salamanders.

supratympanic fold – The ridge following the contour of the typanum.

tadpole – The aquatic, larval form of a frog. It is also known as pollywog.

tail autotomy – The ability to detach the tail as a form of predator escape. The tail grows back in many species.

tetrapod – A four-legged animal.

tubercle – A small protuberance on the surface of the body.

tympanic membrane – The membrane covering the external opening of the tympanum.

tympanum – The eardrum. In amphibians, only present in frogs.

urostyle – The two fused lower vertebrae serving as the origin for jumping muscles in frogs.

vent – Another name for cloaca.

venter – Underside of an animal.

vernal pool – A seasonally ephemeral body of water.

vocal sac – Inflatable pouch on male frogs used to force air over vocal cords.

Suggested Further Reading

Amos, William H. *The Life of the Pond*. New York: McGraw-Hill Book Company, 1967.

Behler, John L., and King, Wayne F. *The Audubon Society Field Guide to North American Reptile and Amphibians*. New York: Alfred A. Knopf, 1979.

Calhoun, Aram J. K., and Klemens, Michael W. *Best Development Practices, Conserving Pool-Breeding Amphibians in Residential and Commercial Developments in the Northeastern United States*. New York: Metropolitan Conservation Alliance, 2002.

Caduto, Michael J. *Pond and Brook, A Guide to Nature in Freshwater Environments*. Massachusetts: Univerity Press of New England, 1985.

Colburn, Elizabeth A. *Vernal Pools, Natural History and Conservation*. Virginia: The McDonald and Woodward Publishing Company, 2004.

Conant, Roger, and Collins, Joseph T. *Reptiles and Amphibians, Eastern/Central North America*. Peterson Field Guides. Boston: Houghton Mifflin Company, 1991.

Dickerson, Mary C. *The Frog Book, North American Toads and Frogs*. New York: Dover Publications, Inc., 1969.

Hausman, Leon A. *Beginner's Guide to Fresh-water Life*. New York: G. P. Putnam Sons, 1950.

Himmelman, John. *A Salamander's Life*. New York: Scholastic, Inc./Children's Press, Inc, 1998.

Himmelman, John. *A Wood Frog's Life*. New York: Scholastic, Inc./Children's Press, Inc., 1998.

Kenney, Leo P., and Burne, Matthew R. *A Field Guide to the Animals of Vernal Pools*. Massachusetts: Massachusetts Division of Fisheries and Wildlife and Vernal Pool Association, 2000.

Kenney, Leo P. *Wicked Big Puddles*. Massachusetts: Reading Memorial High School, Vernal Pool Association, New England Regional Office of the U.S. Environmental Protection Agency, 1995.

Klemens, Michael W. *Amphibians and Reptiles of Connecticut and Adjacent Regions*. Connecticut: State Geological and Natural History Survey of Connecticut, 1993.

Needham, James G., and Needham, Paul R. *A Guide to the Study of Fresh-Water Biology*. San Francisco: Holden-Day, Inc., 1962.

Petranka, James W. *Salamanders of the United States and Canada*. Washington and London: Smithsonian Institution Press, 1998.

Reid, George K. *Pond Life, A Guide to the Common Plants and Animals of North American Ponds and Lakes*. New York: Golden Press, 1967.

Tyning, Thomas F. *A Guide to Amphibians and Reptiles*. Stokes Nature Guides. Boston: Little, Brown and Company, 1990.

Wright, Albert Hazen, and Wright, Anna Allen. *Handbook of Frogs and Toads of United States and Canada*. New York: Comstock Publishing Company, Inc., 1949.

Zim, Herbert S., and Smith, Hobart M. *Reptiles and Amphibians, A Guide to Familiar American Species*. New York: Simon and Schuster, 1953.

Herpetology Organizations and Web Sites

New Jersey
The New Jersey Herpetological Society, P.O. Box 453, Howell, NJ 07731

New York
Long Island Herpetological Society, 476 North Ontario Avenue, Lindenhurst, NY 11757, www.lihs.org

Western New York Herpetological Society, 1372 Lexington Avenue, North Tonawanda, NY 14120, www.wnyherp.org

Pennsylvania
Philadelphia Herp Society, P.O. Box 52261, Philadelphia, PA 19115, www.herpetology.com/phs.html

Northeast Pennsylvania Herpetological Society, 55 W. Luzerne Ave, Larksville, PA 18704, http://www.kingsnake.com/nepa

The Lehigh Valley Herpetological Society, http://members.tripod.com/~lvhs

Connecticut

Connecticut Amphibians, www.ctamphibians.com (author's site)
The Connecticut Herpetologists League, www.kingsnake.com/chl
New England Herpetologist, www.newenglandherper.org
Southern New England Herpetological Association, 2325 Burr Street,
    Fairfield, CT 06430-1806, www.scinax.com/sneha/home.html

Massachusetts

New England Herpetological Society, P.O. Box 1082 Boston, MA 02103,
    www.neherp.com/index.html

Rhode Island

Rhode Island Herpetological Society, 30 Metropolitan Road, Providence, RI
    02908

New Hampshire

New Hampshire Herpetological Society, P.O. Box 4020, Concord, NH
    03302

Vermont

Vermont Herpetological Society Online, www.vermontherps.org

Maine

Maine Herpetological Society, 99 Water Street, Millinocket, ME 04462,
    www.maineherp.org

National Herpetology Organizations:

Amphibian Conservation Alliance, www.frogs.org/index.asp
FrogWeb: Amphibian Declines and Malformations, http://www.frogweb.gov
National Amphibian Research and Monitoring Initiative,
    http://armi.usgs.gov
North American Amphibian Monitoring Program,
    www.pwrc.usgs.gov/naamp/index.html
Partners in Amphibian and Reptile Conservation, Amphibian Conservation
    Alliance, 1700 N. Moore Street, Suite 2000, Arlington, VA 22209,
    www.parcplace.org

Checklist of the Amphibians of the Northeast

Salamanders

__ Marbled salamander *Ambystoma opacum*   NY, CT, RI, MA, VT, NH, ME

__ Jefferson salamander *Ambystoma jeffersonianum*   NY, CT, MA, VT, NH

__ Blue-spotted salamander *Ambystoma laterale*   NY, CT, MA, VT, NH, ME

__ Spotted salamander
Ambystoma maculatum   NY, CT, RI, MA, VT, NH, ME

__ Eastern tiger salamander *Ambystoma tigrinum*   NY

__ Eastern hellbender *Cryptobranchus alleganiensis*   NY

__ Northern dusky salamander
Desmognathus fuscus   NY, CT, RI, MA, VT, NH, ME

__ Allegheny mtn. dusky salamander *Desmognathus ochrophaeus*   NY

__ Northern redback salamander
Plethodon cinereus   NY, CT, RI, MA, VT, NH, ME

__ Northern slimy salamander *Plethodon glutinosus*   NY, CT, NH

__ Wehrle's Salamander *Plethodon wehrlei*   NY

__ Four-toed salamander
Hemidactylium scutatum   NY, CT, RI, MA, VT, NH, ME

__ Northern spring salamander
Gyrinophilus porphyriticus   NY, CT, RI, MA, VT, NH, ME

__ Northern red salamander *Pseudotriton ruber*   NY

__ Northern two-lined salamander
Eurycea bislineata   NY, CT, RI, MA, VT, NH, ME

__ Long-tailed salamander *Eurycea l. longicauda*   NY

__ Red-spotted newt
Notophthalmus viridescens   NY, CT, RI, MA, VT, NH, ME

__ Northern mudpuppy *Necturus maculosus*   NY, CT, RI, MA, VT, NH, ME

Frogs

__	Eastern spadefoot toad *Scaphiopus holbrookii*	NY, CT, RI, MA
__	American toad *Bufo americanus*	NY, CT, RI, MA, VT, NH, ME
__	Fowler's toad *Bufo fowleri*	NY, CT, RI, MA, VT, NH
__	Northern cricket frog *Acris crepitans*	NY
__	Gray treefrog *Hyla versicolo*	NY, CT, RI, MA, VT, NH, ME
__	Spring peeper *Pseudacris crucifer*	NY, CT, RI, MA, VT, NH, ME
__	Western chorus frog *Pseudacris triseriata*	NY, VT
__	Bullfrog *Rana catesbeiana*	NY, CT, RI, MA, VT, NH, ME
__	Green frog *Rana clamitans*	NY, CT, RI, MA, VT, NH, ME
__	Mink frog *Rana septentrionalis*	NY, VT, NH, ME
__	Pickerel frog *Rana palustris*	NY, CT, RI, MA, VT, NH, ME
__	Northern leopard frog *Rana pipiens*	NY, CT, RI, MA, VT, NH, ME
__	Southern leopard frog *Rana sphenocephala utricularius*	NY
__	Wood frog *Rana sylvatica*	NY, CT, RI, MA, VT, NH, ME

Index

(Page numbers in **boldface** refer to photos or illustrations;
numbers **P1** through **P24** are color photo insert pages)